P9-DMR-859

PRESENTED TO:

OPA GERHARDT

FROM:

MONICA & family

DATE:

JUNE 15/2019

10
MINUTES
IN THE WORD

Psalms

ZONDERVAN

10 Minutes in the Word: Psalms

Copyright © 2018 Zondervan

This title is also available as a Zondervan ebook.

Requests for information should be addressed to:

Zondervan, 3900 Sparks Dr. SE, Grand Rapids, Michigan 49546

Library of Congress Cataloging-in-Publication Data
ISBN 978-0-310-09125-7

Scripture quotations are taken from the Holy Bible, New International Version®, NIV®. Copyright © 1973, 1978, 1984, 2011 by Biblica, Inc.® Used by permission of Zondervan. All rights reserved worldwide. www.zondervan .com. The "NIV" and "New International Version" are trademarks registered in the United States Patent and Trademark Office by Biblica, Inc.®

Any Internet addresses (websites, blogs, etc.) and telephone numbers in this book are offered as a resource. They are not intended in any way to be or imply an endorsement by Zondervan, nor does Zondervan vouch for the content of these sites and numbers for the life of this book.

All rights reserved. No part of this publication may be reproduced, stored in a retrieval system, or transmitted in any form or by any means—electronic, mechanical, photocopy, recording, or any other—except for brief quotations in printed reviews, without the prior permission of the publisher.

Art direction: Kathy Mitchell
Interior design: Kristy Edwards

Printed in China

18 19 20 21 22   TIMS   10 9 8 7 6 5 4 3 2 1

Contents

Introduction

T he book of Psalms is a collection of prayers, poems, and songs that focus the believer's thoughts on praising God and reveling in His Word. It is a collection of at least six authors.[1] David is thought to have written approximately seventy-three psalms, making him the main contributor.[2] Psalms is a glimpse into the amazing life of David, a man and king after God's own heart. The psalms are intimately personal and explore the whole realm of human emotion: from deep despair to ecstatic delight; from a yearning for vengeance to a spirit of humility and forgiveness; from earnest pleading to God for protection to jubilant praise for His deliverance. Through the entire book, however, the writers express their serene confidence in God's guidance and provision.

The psalms are loved and memorized by so many because of their relatability in addressing many of life's most significant questions. We want to be reassured of God's presence in our everyday lives and learn how to praise God regardless of our circumstances. The book of Psalms provides a sanctuary where our questions and spiritual yearnings can be recognized—a place where we are reminded of God's sovereignty and grace.

The Firm Counsel of God

You, Lord, are a shield around me,
  my glory, the One who lifts my head high.
I call out to the Lord,
  and he answers me from his holy mountain.

I lie down and sleep;
  I wake again, because the Lord sustains me.
I will not fear though tens of thousands
  assail me on every side.

Arise, Lord!
  Deliver me, my God!
Strike all my enemies on the jaw;
  break the teeth of the wicked.
—*Psalm 3:3–7*

T here has never been a time before when advice and instruction could be so easily found. Everywhere we turn in this era of instant access we are confronted with advice. Advice has its own industry and it often points us to ourselves, to look inward for self-help. But the book of Psalms opens with an invitation to consider two different sources of counsel. The counsel of the world offers advice that may seem dazzling and clever, even well-informed and intellectual, but it is unsettled. The counsel of the world does not point toward an unquestionable or established end, nor does it encourage walking by any firm and fixed instruction. In contrast, we are encouraged that blessed and prosperous are the souls who delight in the Word of God, who meditate on it day and night, who take up the yoke of His mandates. They shall be like a tree, fruitful and flourishing—fully equipped for every good work and better suited to face the challenges of life.

David was commissioned by God to be king, and he was competent in every way, but the enemies of God and His anointed are numerous. They struggle against His restraints, shudder at His obligations, and bristle at His commandments. They will not be governed. David's own son Absalom had won the hearts of many of his followers. Together, they conspired against his father and their king. Not only did Absalom desire David's crown, he also wanted to kill him. David fled for his life. Barefoot, with his head covered in mourning, he ascended the Mount of Olives. He wept and prayed. Many were saying David's life was in such ruins that not even God could save him. The counsel he was receiving was unsettled, beckoning him to be swayed to and fro, but David tuned his heart to the firm counsel of God.

Are you facing provocation and torment from people close to you, those you have good reason to expect love, gratitude, and respect from instead? Maybe you are at your wits' end, having seemingly lost all you know to be true and all you hold dear. The unsettled counsel of this world is surely surrounding you and may be springing up within your own heart, advising you to escape or turn inward. You might be tempted to give up, feeling as if you can't trust anyone, not even God. You might be convinced He cannot deliver you. Don't give up or give in! Instead, like David, let your distress and grief drive you to the Mount of Olives.

Lord, Your assurances are a shield wrapped around me. Lift my head and remove its mourning shroud. Soothe the soles of my bare feet. Counsel me from Your throne. Arise, O King, over all that threatens me today and save me. When I lie down to sleep tonight, make me dwell in Your safety, and sustain me in Your perfect rest.

Weep and pray. Weep and sing. Weep and believe.

A Beggar at God's Throne

LORD, do not rebuke me in your anger
    or discipline me in your wrath.
Have mercy on me, LORD, for I am faint;
    heal me, LORD, for my bones are in agony.
My soul is in deep anguish.
    How long, LORD, how long? . . .

I am worn out from my groaning.
All night long I flood my bed with weeping
    and drench my couch with tears.
—*Psalm 6:1–3, 6*

P salm 7 is described as a *shiggaion* of David. A *shiggaion* is a wandering song or a wild and passionate ode.[3] David sang this prayer to the Lord concerning Cush, a Benjamite. King Saul, who once employed David with high rank, grew jealous of his military successes and the transfer of the adoration and praise of his people. Saul began to fear David because the blessing of the Lord was with David and had left Saul. Cush was likely some kinsman of Saul who had given a false account of David, further provoking Saul's anger against him. David took this insult and injury to the Lord and was not rattled by it, nor was he discouraged. He was composed and maybe even a little cheerful. The more David's enemies sought to find fault in him, the more he resolved himself to not only avoid sin, but to avoid all appearances of sin. In the same way, let the injuries you receive from others set a match to your devotions rather than letting it kindle an uncontrollable fire. Settle yourself to be above reproach.

David made praying his career. He committed to pray in the morning when he was fresh and not yet steeped in the obligations of the day. Just as a priest in the temple would lay out wood for the daily sacrifice, David also prepared himself. David's prayers were often crying prayers to a hearing God. Your confidants may be far away, but God ever has an ear inclined to His children. He will take your prayers into consideration. He will sift them through His divine and compassionate wisdom, and in His timing, return a tenderhearted answer of peace. Are you sick? Sick in spirit? Sick in rebellion? Have your troubles been heavy and long? Have your eyes been consumed with grief? Rest easy for your God is the Great Physician of body, mind, and soul. Pray, confident your Father is concerned for the frame He created for you and is aware of all its maladies. Pray, knowing those who cry and sow in tears are getting ready to harvest God's abundant mercy. And pray with a penetrating fear of God's displeasure, which we should dread most of all. Prayers of all sickness soon will give way to praise in healing, victory in suffering, thankfulness in forgiveness of sin, and assured triumph against those who persecute you.

Lord, I am thrown flat down, stretched and gaping. Examine me from head to toe for defects, explore my heart for sorrow, frisk my spirit for shortcomings. Bend Your hearing ear to consider my case and do what seems good to You. Let my prayers be hallowed and glorified in Your Name. The head of my belief already knows Your peace. The eye of my faith already sees Your harvest of unspeakable joy.

Rise in the morning to be a beggar at God's throne. Go and fetch fresh supplies of mercy and grace for the day.

His Watchful Eye

You, God, see the trouble of the afflicted;
　　you consider their grief and take it in hand.
The victims commit themselves to you;
　　you are the helper of the fatherless. . . .

You, LORD, hear the desire of the afflicted;
　　you encourage them, and you listen to their cry,
defending the fatherless and the oppressed,
　　so that mere earthly mortals
　　will never again strike terror.
—*Psalm 10:14, 17–18*

D oesn't it seem as though the bad guys often have an easy life and get away with lawlessness while the good guys often struggle just to survive and get through life? Sometimes it seems as if it doesn't benefit us to be and do good when the evil prosper and the righteous suffer hardship and adversity. David understood this frustration well. Although he was anointed king as a teenager, he spent much of his twenties running and hiding from the ungodly and wicked King Saul. On many occasions, David could have ended his own misery by killing Saul, but chose to do the right thing and spared his life, only to watch him return to his decadent palace and vengeful mission, while David returned to his cave and life on the run.

David often began his prayers determined to praise and acknowledge the Lord while still in the teeth of his trials. When the bad guys win, he submitted to God. He took time to reflect on the vastness and wonder of God. He noticed and recognized all of nature's complexity, God's wisdom, creativity, and majesty. He knew his God is a God who far transcends His awe-inspiring creation, but has remarkably crowned humankind His greatest work of art and most valuable treasure. David marked remembrances of God's faithfulness in the past because recalling the memory of one mercy often refreshes the memory of numerous others. In so doing, David could take comfort and put his trust in the blessed assurance of God's future justice. He moved freely between a cry of oppression to a song of loyalty, even in the hardest of times, when God seems far-off and silent.

It can be difficult to watch the wicked of this world prosper while justice seems to escape the good and steadfast. Take refuge in the promise that God is in His holy temple and on His heavenly throne. Nothing of this world ever escapes His watchful eye. Consider all the works of His hand and stand in awe of His immeasurable power and limitless strength. Find solace in knowing He is righteous and loves justice. Remember His merciful deliverance and fair judgment thus far. Anticipate by faith and trust with sanctified gladness, God's final verdict and victory over all inequity, corruption, cruelty, and every evil misdeed.

Lord, I marvel at all Your hands have made. Who am I that the God of all creation is mindful of me? As high and lofty as You are, I can hardly fathom Your esteem of me. Lord, I will rejoice and be glad in You. I will put my faith and trust in You, believing You are on Your throne. Even though the wicked prosper and the evil go free, no person or activity eludes Your supreme justice. Therefore, I will take refuge in You and wait patiently for Your promised verdict.

One day, every wrong will be made right and all tears will be wiped away.

Pour Out Your Heart to God

How long, LORD? Will you forget me forever?
  How long will you hide your face from me?
How long must I wrestle with my thoughts
    and day after day have sorrow in my heart?
  How long will my enemy triumph over me?
—*Psalm 13:1–2*

D oesn't it feel good to vent all your troubles to a good friend? Even if your problems remain, a load is still somehow lifted when you have the opportunity to lift everything that is weighing you down, up and out of yourself. But sometimes misfortune lingers for a long, long time and tests your patience. It becomes very difficult to stay calm and it's easy to think your tears will last forever, especially when you have no one to talk to or hash out your burdens and anxieties with. You continually try to figure out what to do; you run on your own steam, but nothing seems to work out.

David penned many of his psalms during Saul's reign when there was a general decay of honesty, religious reverence, fervor, and devotion. He often complained to God because he so often experienced the treachery of his enemies and found himself lonely in the company of false friends. He howled out his persistent "how long?" inquiry, expressing his mourning over the ever-lingering and ever-returning trials tormenting him. David complained that God had withdrawn from him and delayed to relieve him, so he cried out to God for support. His groans and complaints stirred up his prayers. He longed for the inward solace he once knew. He longed for inner peace—to feel God's presence and reassurance—more than he longed for his problems to go away. Like Jesus, he was crying out, "My God, why hast thou forsaken me?"

As a child of God, you have freedom of speech and can approach the throne of grace in boldness. You have a sympathetic and empathetic friend in Jesus. He is always available and willing to listen to you pour out your heart and vent your frustrations. You can be confident you are hashing out your burdens and anxieties with Someone who truly understands. Jesus knows, firsthand, the afflictions and tribulations of this world. He has experienced the treachery of enemies and has found Himself lonely in the company of false friends. He knows what it feels like when God hides His face and leaves Him in the dark.

Lord, the familiar repeated cries of my prayers are a very howling in my soul. Return Yourself to me that I might see Your face again. I long for You even more than I long for my problems to go away. Thank You for the reassurance of Your understanding. Jesus, I find great peace knowing You have walked in my shoes down these same paths before me.

Sing your song of lament, but end with joy and triumph. Your deliverance is as good as finished.

He Is Your Portion

LORD, you alone are my portion and my cup;
   you make my lot secure.
The boundary lines have fallen for me in pleasant
      places;
   surely I have a delightful inheritance.
—*Psalm 16:5-6*

D o you ever feel like an outsider? Do you ever feel like a stranger or a straggler, wandering about and scattered when everyone around you seems to have it all together? Are you poor and destitute in mind or spirit? Maybe you are just flat broke in every way. Take comfort, for the sanctuary of God moves from place to place in the middle of the desert of this broken world. The tabernacle of God has open doors and is calling and ever welcoming to those who are lost and weary. It is not a fort with armed men guarding the entrance, and yet those within are defended from the heat of the sun and take refuge from the storm. Take hope, for the people of God do wander as strangers and stragglers in the wilderness of this world, afflicted on every side, persecuted from one place to the next. They never settle into a place of constant and sound rest. The follower of Christ is surely a pilgrim here on earth.

However, David, who knew well the reality of wandering, declared the Lord as his portion and the Lord as greater than all of heaven and earth. Earth is just a minuscule point compared to the immense vastness of the universe, and the universe is just a minute, microscopic point compared to the limitless, measureless, and boundless Lord. Jesus, Himself, had no desire to seek or hunt after any other gods because His cup was already full. He looked only to God for preservation, protection, and deliverance, and David would not have been called a man after God's own heart if he did not do the same. He flew to prayer in all times of need. Both David and our Lord and Savior Jesus Christ, often penniless, dirt-poor, and surrounded by danger, sought refuge in God's sanctuary and trusted God only for deliverance. They took comfort in the promise of their delightful inheritance.

It is no wonder the child of God often seems so peculiar, odd, and hard to understand to the people of this world. Nor is it any wonder the child of God often feels like an itinerant drifter, a rambling nomad. Though our journey takes us to earth, this is not our home. The children of God are following Jesus, moving through the wilderness, making our way to a fixed hill. Though some may prosper much in this world, it is nothing compared to what we have in Christ. There is nothing in this whole world compared to all He is. And He is your portion.

Lord, how shallow is the cup of my struggles and sorrows when compared to the deep cup of Your unending love and promises. No greater mercy can I find but for You to dwell with me here, to be my full portion, as You lead me to Your holy hill to dwell with You forever.

However poor your condition is on this journey, Jesus is your guide and full, nourishing ration. Yearn to possess more of Him, but not more than Him.

He Is Your Rock

You, Lord, keep my lamp burning;
　　my God turns my darkness into light.
With Your help I can advance against a troop;
　　with my God I can scale a wall.

As for God, His way is perfect:
　　The Lord's word is flawless;
　　he shields all who take refuge in him.
For who is God besides the Lord?
　　And who is the Rock except our God?
—Psalm 18:28–31

P salm 18 is often referred to as the grateful retrospect.[4] The title says David sang this song to the Lord when the Lord delivered him from the hand of all his enemies, including Saul. This psalm is written after Saul's death in the period just before David, at long last, ascends the throne to become Israel's king. Since the moment God declared David would be the future king of Israel, he faced nothing but trouble and hardship. In fact, he spent twenty years on the run as a fugitive and lost everything. He spent his youth running, fighting, and hiding in caves. He lost all his comforts, his family, and his connection and relationships with his own people. At times, he even lost his close relationship with God.

Now Saul was dead and David was about to be king. He sat down, looked back, and wrote a love letter to God. He not only thanked God for rescuing him, but also for all God had done for him while in the midst of his many adversities. In the end, he was thankful for his difficult journey thus far, for it had made him the man he had become. He knew the years of trouble had done something good and necessary in his life and prepared him for what was to come. In grateful retrospect, he knew his faith had been tested because what he used to know and believe by faith, he now knew through personal experience.

God had brought David to the throne and given him light to rule. After twenty years fighting through darkness, he wasn't overcome or exhausted, but supernaturally strengthened. David spoke of the great things he could do empowered by God, but marveled at God's perfect plan and perfect way. God had proven His character and the character of His Word. God had never failed David. David passed every test and every word was proven true. David cried out and asked the question, who else but this God of his could be Lord? No others had proven themselves to be true.

The God who came through for David is the same God who can and will come through for you, if you allow yourself to be put in situations where God must prove Himself true to His Word. He is your Rock, where you can find shade from the merciless heat of the desert and shelter in its cracks and crevices. He is your Rock, where you can find a firm footing, an immovable foundation on which to stand and fight.

Lord, I am grateful for the hope I have in You. You are a God of Your Word and always prove faithful. Though I may not yet see my victory, I know it will come and many more afterward. On a solid Rock I stand, and all other ground is sinking sand. Help me to remember I am as good as delivered by the very same faithful God who delivered King David so many years ago.

Are you ready to let go and allow God to prove Himself to you?

Seasons of Drought and Plenty

Through the victories you gave, his glory is great;
    you have bestowed on him splendor and majesty.
Surely you have granted him unending blessings
    and made him glad with the joy of your presence.
For the king trusts in the Lord;
    through the unfailing love of the Most High
    he will not be shaken.
—*Psalm 21:5–7*

Read Psalms 19-21

D oesn't it seem as though as soon as you are rescued from the desert, hydrated, and replenished, the weather forecast predicts record heat waves coming your way? Just when you find yourself warm and snug after being plucked from the tempest sea, storm clouds start to form in the distance? Just when you get a firm footing and catch your breath, the ground starts to rumble? David had finally become king, but even so, he was not spared hassle and unrest. On the contrary, in Psalm 20 we find King David threatened by more difficulties and danger, possibly going to war. This psalm was written as a song of prayer and protection for his people to sing and pray over him because even the greatest of men often find themselves in much trouble, or at least threatened by much trouble.

No doubt King David had many who were praying for his protection, safety, and success. As king, he had prophets, priests, and many good and pious subjects praying for him, and yet, we still see him praying for himself. He knew prosperity was not a reason to relent in his resolve to remain steadfast in his relationship with the Lord, or cease in earnest prayer. He still reflected on the majesty of God's creation and marveled at the glory of God that can easily be seen. He continued to faithfully press into the Book of Scriptures, knowing they contain the will of the Lord for him as king and as His child. He never ceased to acknowledge and praise God for the benefits and mercies he received, thanking God for his victories in full confidence of further success, come what may.

While the Lord desires us to enjoy the seasons of bounty he has graciously and abundantly bestowed upon us, we should resolve ourselves to never forget where our blessings come from and how easily they can be threatened by the Enemy. Jesus assures us that in this world we will have trouble and it is lurking around every corner, threatening to destroy everything the Lord has accomplished for you and in you. Understanding this, observe the farmer: in times of harvest, when his silos, barns, and cellars are overflowing, the farmer is sure to glean new seeds for the next season of replanting. So, too, must we remain diligent in cultivating our relationship with God in seasons of drought and seasons plenty.

Lord, it is hard to remember past hardships when things are going well, let alone think about preparing for hardships that may come. Please remind me to remain steadfast in You, not only when drought is threatening my harvest, but also when my yield is plentiful and overflowing. In my times of abundance, help me remember my growing season on earth will often be threatened by drought and locusts. Teach me to store up my reserves in You.

Is life going pretty well? Be grateful and make it a habit to remember all God has delivered you from so you will not be easily shaken when trouble comes knocking on your door.

God's Guidance

The LORD is my shepherd, I lack nothing.
    He makes me lie down in green pastures,
he leads me beside quiet waters,
    he refreshes my soul.
He guides me along the right paths
    for his name's sake.
Even though I walk
    through the darkest valley,
I will fear no evil,
    for you are with me;
your rod and your staff,
    they comfort me.

—*Psalm 23:1–4*

M y God, my God, why have you forsaken me?" Have you ever felt forsaken by God? Abandoned and disowned? Has your heart ever made a similar plea? It has been said that David was a type of Christ, and in Psalm 22 we see him crying out the very same words Jesus did as He hung on the cross. At the end of the psalm, David closed with words resembling, "It is finished." Many passages within the book of Psalms pertain to David but also have a dual reference to Jesus. There may be no greater example than in Psalm 22, where David speaks fully of the humiliation of Christ crucified followed by His veneration and exultation. While we are reading David's words, we are also somehow seeing a mystical glimpse of our Lord and Savior's saddest hours and hearing His dying words. David's experience is a reflection of both the darkness and the glory of the cross, and through him we can see the same sufferings of Christ and the glory that followed.

Psalm 23 reveals a David who is likely much older at this point in time. There seems to be a fullness and contentment within this psalm that points to an author mellowed by time and his life's experiences. We see him looking back on his childhood as a shepherd boy and his memory of the green valleys, the quiet and gentle streams, and the dark glens where he had led his sheep before. Then later, we see him remembering the fiery years of warfare and rebellion, sin and despair, and through it all recognizing God's gracious presence and guidance. David is able to look back and declare it was all very good and looks forward as he says, "Surely your goodness and love will follow me all the days of my life."

You will also find yourself crying out to God in the same way as both David and Jesus from time to time in this life on earth. First Peter 4:13 says, "But rejoice inasmuch as you participate in the sufferings of Christ, so that you may be overjoyed when his glory is revealed." Rejoice when you suffer for the same reasons Jesus suffered. Rejoice when you suffer in the same way David did, for you are being sanctified through and through and conformed more and more into the likeness of Jesus, your Lord and Savior. In the end, His glory will be revealed to you.

Lord, You are my Shepherd. You lead me through the various pastures of my life. You lead me to rest and You lead me to the work You have for me. And You lead me through the valleys of my sorrow. Lord, You are my Host, and I am a guest at Your table. You provide food and rest for my journey. In You I have hope of a brighter future here on earth, and all my weary wanderings will one day end in the warmth of peace in my Father's house.

Pain and heaviness are mixed with our joy here on earth, but we rejoice in the hope we have of the fullness of pure joy we will enjoy in heaven.

Your Rescuer

Hear my voice when I call, Lord;
   be merciful to me and answer me.
My heart says of you, "Seek his face!"
   Your face, Lord, I will seek.
Do not hide your face from me,
   do not turn your servant away in anger;
   you have been my helper.
Do not reject me or forsake me,
   God my Savior.
Though my father and mother forsake me,
   the Lord will receive me.
—Psalm 27:7–10

A smile of encouragement and approval from God is the greatest reward and comfort a believer can receive, and just the thought of God withdrawing Himself is the greatest misfortune and misery. David had seen Saul, his predecessor, turn away from God in anger. David, knowing and acknowledging his own shortcomings, had every reason to pray and plead that God would not withdraw His grace and mercy from him. Sometimes God may turn away for our own good, that we might flounder and struggle enough to recognize our need to shun our destructive ways, confess our sin, and be led back into the fold to receive God's healing and grace again. David shuddered in fear at the thought of those who turn from God altogether and suffer life without Him, and he wanted nothing to do with that sort of life.

It is the natural course within a family that a father and mother, while yet deeply loving their children, send them out to take care of and provide for themselves when they become young adults. When their children are young, they lead them by the hand, but when they are grown, they let go and let them stand on their own two feet. However, when trouble comes, they are still available. Sometimes parents find themselves in situations where, though they would like to help their grown children, for some reason beyond their control they are not able. Maybe distance or lack of finances hinders them. In these situations, the Lord takes them up into His good care and keeping just as He opened the spring for Ishmael and provided baby Moses with a savior in Pharaoh's own daughter.

Then there are times when not only parents, but all the people we would expect to be there for us till the very end forsake us when we need them the most. Some of the greatest people in the Bible were cast out of their families and communities. They were often persecuted and falsely accused. When this happened to David, he appealed to the Supreme Judge. He pleaded his case in good conscience and his mighty God came to his rescue, supported his good cause, lifted him up from his gloom, and gave him victory over his enemies. This all-powerful God is the advocate and comfort to the persecuted and the steadfast and loving Father of the orphan.

Lord, You are my light and salvation—whom shall I fear? Lord, You are the stronghold of my life—of whom shall I be afraid? You sit enthroned above the storms and floods of my life so when my enemies advance against me and my friends and family forsake me, You will give me strength and bless me with peace.

Does it seem as though it's you against the whole world? Remember: if God is on your side, who can rise against you?

Grace and Pardon

When I kept silent,
   my bones wasted away
   through my groaning all day long.
For day and night
   your hand was heavy on me;
my strength was sapped
   as in the heat of summer.

Then I acknowledged my sin to you
   and did not cover up my iniquity.
I said, "I will confess
   my transgressions to the Lord."
And you forgave
   the guilt of my sin.

—Psalm 32:3–5

Read Psalms 30–33

H ave you ever gotten yourself into a big pickle? Dug yourself a hole so big you couldn't climb out? We can recognize in the story of David's life, rising hills of confidence and triumph, but also many valleys of mourning and despair. Often, he found himself in valleys of transgression through no fault of his own. He fell into the pits others had dug for him. Other times, he dug those pits himself. Sometimes he willfully stayed in those pits, foolishly attempting to hide himself from an all seeing God until his silence made him physically and emotionally ill. He could not rest easy for long, as the excessive fears and sorrow made him weary and the continual burden on his conscience made his bones ache. He resolved that he could no longer live like that and poured his guts out. He openly and honestly, with great regret, confessed all his sins, acknowledged all the trouble they had caused him, and humbly asked for clemency. These psalms teach us, over and over, the only path to forgiveness and a peaceful conscience is regretful confession and acknowledgment of the justice in the consequences and correction we receive, knowing full well we deserve much harsher punishment.

When God extends His hand that you might grab hold of Him so He can lift you out of the holes you dig for yourself, make it a habit to not only praise Him in thankfulness, but also to remember your duties as a child of God. When you find yourself forgiven, on a hill of confidence and triumph, remember how you felt and all the complaints you had when you were in your valley of mourning and despair. Let those uncomfortable memories spur you to govern yourself well and never go there again! But when you falter, rush to confess your sin and praise God for His grace and pardon.

There is this peculiar favor God extends to His children. We often hold on to our grudges and struggle to forgive those who wrong us, but God is ever at the ready to extend His hand of peace, His arms of warmth, His heart of love, and His spirit of forgiveness—over and over and over again. We find it easy to trust God when we continually acknowledge His justice, His goodness, His truth, and His sovereign providence appearing in our own lives and in the works of His creation.

Lord, it is easy to sing to You joyful praises when I think back on all the times You have delivered me from all the trouble I've gotten myself into. Please nudge my heart in remembrance. Remind me of how bad I feel when I'm trying to hide from You in my sin. Please knead my heart into softness when things are going well. Keep me pliable and humble so I will not have to be brought into submission like a stubborn mule.

Pardon soon follows earnest confession and repentance, and God's mercy is glorified.

Fear of the Lord

This poor man called, and the LORD heard him;
    he saved him out of all his troubles.
The angel of the LORD encamps around those who
        fear him,
    and he delivers them.

Taste and see that the LORD is good;
    blessed is the one who takes refuge in him.
Fear the LORD, you his holy people,
    for those who fear him lack nothing.
—Psalm 34:6–9

Doesn't it seem as if being encouraged to fear God must be some sort of a typo? If God loves us and wants good things for us, then why should we fear him? While the "fear of God" actually does suggest an apprehension of divine punishment, the fear of the Lord we are generally called to consider is a specific sense of respect, awe, and submission to God.

When we look at David's backstory, we don't really see this full sense of respect, awe, and submission to God. There was a time when Saul sent men to apprehend and kill David at his home. David fled through a window and Michal, David's wife, took an idol and laid it on the bed as a decoy. When Saul's men came for him, she said he was ill so that David might get away with a good head start. Another time, David was expected to sit at Saul's table for a feast, but he asked his friend Jonathan to lie to his father about David's absence. Imprisoned, he faked insanity to gain release. David once fled from Saul to a city called Nob and lied to a priest named Ahimelech, saying Saul had commissioned him to carry out an urgent task. David requested provisions and a weapon. Ahimelech gave him some of the consecrated bread and the sword David had taken from Goliath. When Saul heard of the favor David had received in Nob, he commanded that eighty-four priests, including Ahimelech, be executed. Not only the priests, but also every man, woman, and child. David later acknowledged his deception was indeed costly, as he was morally responsible for the massacre at Nob.

During this time, David approached all his problems in a down-to-earth and practical way, and deception and violence became his way of dealing with his fear. It seemed acceptable and made perfect sense if it was done to preserve his life and help make him feel safe and secure. However, in Psalm 34 we see David recognizing that his biggest problem was that he feared man in these situations more than he feared God. In other psalms of David, we see him encourage us not to fret about the prosperity of the wicked, but to remember their soon and sure destruction. And he calls us to focus on all the good and victory God has in store for those who trust Him.

You might not resort to deception and violence, but do you often find yourself focusing on what others have done or might do to you or what might happen? Do you try your best to run or hide, but continue to worry and fret? If so, you might not be living with a full sense of respect, awe, and submission to God. Endeavor to remain loyal and patiently leave the situation with God.

Lord, search my heart and show me all the ways I fear others and fear my circumstances more than I trust in You. Remind me again and again how big You are and how small and weak my afflictions are in comparison to Your power and strength. Teach me to diligently follow Your ways and believe You when You say You will come to my rescue every single time.

No matter how bleak it may look right now, trust it will all be well for those who fear the Lord.

But a Breath

Show me, Lord, my life's end
   and the number of my days;
   let me know how fleeting my life is.
You have made my days a mere handbreadth;
   the span of my years is as nothing before you.
Everyone is but a breath,
   even those who seem secure.

Surely everyone goes around like a mere phantom;
   in vain they rush about, heaping up wealth
   without knowing whose it will finally be.
—*Psalm 39:4-6*

They say life is short for a very good reason . . . it is! Since life is so short and our lives are so temporary, how can we make the most of it? Often, we are too distracted to contemplate this question, but when seasons change or halting events take place, we settle down into a more pensive frame of mind. We can't believe how fast time has flown when our toddlers are suddenly old enough to start school. We blink just a few more times and we're dropping them off at college. Blink again and we're watching them drive away on their honeymoon. We focus our attention on career goals and setting ourselves up financially, and before we know it our youth is gone and we realize we're going to have to scale down our bucket lists. As soon as we take the Christmas tree down, we're closing out one year and beginning another. Before we know it, summer is over and the holiday season is rapidly approaching.

Psalm 39 reveals a time when David, painfully aware of the shortness of life, had fallen ill and he began to wrestle with these thoughts. Scripture often mentions how we are here today and gone tomorrow. Psalm 90:5–6 describes humanity as grass, glistening and new in the morning, but dried up and blown away by evening. These can be rather depressing thoughts, but David reminded us to look at life with an eternal perspective. He compared his short life to God in eternity. When we're young, one hundred years seems like a very long time, a whole lifetime if we're lucky. But when we view the fleeting years of human life in the light of God and eternity, they are just a vapor.

You might be asking yourself, *So what now? Life is short and death is certain. What can I do about it?* You have two choices. You can live for yourself and go back to that whirlwind of hustle and bustle. You can eat, drink, and be merry as long as you are able, or you can live your life for the Lord, which is the only option with any hope. Catching yourself before you get swept up in the distractions of life and pursuing personal holiness will keep you levelheaded and centered. Receiving God's discipline as lessons to be learned and applied and pursuing Christ above all else will help you live this transient life to its fullest.

Lord, it is so easy to forget the lessons I learn as soon as my suffering has passed. It's so easy for me to become lost in the chaos and return to the mind-set that life will just keep on going for a very long time. Help me remember how short life is and that I will not find comfort, peace, and happiness by chasing after them, but only by seeking You. You are the very source of all good things, here and in eternity.

Because life is so short and our assignment here is temporary, we will find contentment and purpose if we live our lives for the Lord in the light of eternity.

Thirsting for God's Presence

As the deer pants for streams of water,
so my soul pants for you, my God.
My soul thirsts for God, for the living God.
When can I go and meet with God?
—*Psalm 42:1-2*

A re you longing for resilience? In light of everything that demands your physical and mental attention, your desire is to toughen up and bounce back quickly so you might be ready to tackle the next challenge. You decide to reduce your screen time, disconnect, shake off the overstimulation, and equalize on a cognitive level. When one project has you blocked, you decide to switch gears and work on another for a while, giving your brain a chance to recharge before returning your attention back to the difficult task or situation. You spend time outdoors in the sunshine, seeking some respite. You tell yourself if you can just make it to Friday or if you can just make it to that upcoming vacation, you'll let everything go, reenergize, and find rejuvenation. You push through with all you have left, but when you crawl into bed or when the weekend comes, you can't stop thinking about the problems that need to be worked through. You can't seem to shut your brain off completely, even on vacation, because those unfinished tasks or unresolved problems are just going to be waiting for you when you get home.

David's story shows us a man who spent a good portion of his youth on the run from place to place, hiding out from his enemies who sought his demise. We now see an older man who had many responsibilities as king. The decisions he made would not only affect himself, but a whole nation. Running and hiding from his enemies did not soothe him because they were always there again. Pushing through on his own steam and depending on his own knowledge did not ease his stress or build his confidence as king over his people. In all these places and in all these situations, David remembered God. Even when he could no longer enjoy the fellowship of his people, he lifted his heart and kept communion with his Lord. David did not seek comfort or honor, but friendship and closeness with God. This connection wasn't just an aside or a luxury in his life, but an absolute necessity. Like a parched traveler whose canteen is empty, a body scorched through drought, or a deer who pants for streams of water, his very soul thirsted for the presence of God.

While you seek to balance your life by changing your habits horizontally, don't forget the vertical. Look up, for your resilience, your ability to bounce back quickly, to find respite and lasting energy, is found in the strength of your Lord.

Lord, I have heard of all You did through David and others. You drove out nations and You made Your people flourish. It was not by their sword that they found victory; it was Your right hand and the light of Your face, for You loved them. When I am out of balance and overwhelmed, let me not attempt to approach my circumstances simply with practical solutions, but to examine my spirit. I am often in want simply because my persecuted and parched soul pants for You.

When you are overwhelmed or depressed, while searching for relief, don't forget your main need is to seek and hunt for God.

The God of Refuge

There is a river whose streams make glad the city of
    God,
  the holy place where the Most High dwells.
God is within her, she will not fall;
  God will help her at break of day.
Nations are in uproar, kingdoms fall;
  he lifts his voice, the earth melts. . . .

He says, "Be still, and know that I am God;
  I will be exalted among the nations,
  I will be exalted in the earth."
—*Psalm 46:4–6, 10*

T he three psalms in today's reading all reveal dual referencing. Psalm 45 is an *epithalamium*, a song celebrating a marriage.[5] On one hand, it seems to be a royal wedding song written and sung for a Jewish king on the day of his wedding to a foreign woman. But on the other hand, it recognizes the mystical marriage between Christ and His church. It speaks of the royal Bridegroom, who is Christ, His utmost excellence, the glory of His victories, the goodness of His governing, and the splendor of His court. The royal bride's (the church's) consent is gained, then the wedding, and afterward the reproduction of those who will go out into all the nations, professing the gospel of Christ, enlarging the family of Christ.

Psalm 47 is a song sung during the Jewish Feast of Trumpets addressing a historical victory, but is also a foreshadowing of God coming down in the person of His Son, Jesus Christ, to dwell among us. Further, it is a foreshadowing of Jesus' return at the end of the age. In every case, the very dwelling presence and full deliverance from Jesus Christ our Lord brings the promise of such immeasurable joy it easily brings us to march in triumph and praise Him openly and loudly!

In Psalm 46 we see a city of God, the holy place where the Most

High dwells. The people of this city are always glad because there is a river with many streams flowing into the city. One of the best defenses against an invading army is a guaranteed water source within its walls. The Lord of hosts dwells in the city and His presence, blessing, and provision keep the city safe even when the earth moves violently underneath. He pays no attention to raging nations because He is the Commander of His people and of His armies in heaven. When He speaks, everyone stops in their tracks. The whole earth is still.

Just as the God of all creation and the King of all kings has meticulously ordered the universe and the plan of humankind, He is also your devoted, loving Father and has meticulously designed you for His specific and providential purposes. In other words, He has written down goals for your life, and He will not desert you or stop working them out in you until the day you meet Him face-to-face, wholly complete according to His perfect plan.

Lord, as a finite being it is so hard for me to wrap my mind around Your infinite ways. Thank You for Your divine Word, for it lays it all out in layman's terms, giving my mind a glimpse of Your glory, greatness, and providence. I'm thinking about all the times I've doubted You and realizing how futile it's been to argue with You, for the whole universe is ordered and obedient to Your voice.

The God of Jacob is the same God of your refuge, by covenant, but also by mercy and grace. Be still and know!

The Security of the Church

As we have heard,
   so we have seen
in the city of the LORD Almighty,
   in the city of our God:
God makes her secure
   forever.
—*Psalm 48:8*

A re you wary of attending and joining a local church? If you have a home church, are you often tempted to stay on the sidelines or skip services when life becomes chaotic and you feel as if you need to focus your time on other important matters? Does it seem as though the church is becoming less and less relevant anyway? A bit old-fashioned for the times we live in?

When we examine Psalm 48, we observe the splendor of the city of Jerusalem. The people would come from all over the country to the city. They would make a pilgrimage to offer their sacrifices, to serve God, and to praise and worship Him, knowing He would receive them and give them a blessing in return. In Jerusalem God was known, He was great among them, and they were devoted to Him. It was the city appointed to Him for sincere and heartfelt service and worship, and in that city God was greatly praised. When nations rallied around it, they turned back in fear because they recognized the holiness of God protected the city. It was under His special favor and protection, and He caused its enemies to suffer throes of pain, as a woman in childbirth.

In this picture of the holy city, we see the bride of Christ, the church, the tabernacle of God among men, highly favored and profoundly loved by God. The same great things He did in Jerusalem,

He is also doing for His church. Let our faith be strengthened and let our hope be sure of the stability and security of the church. God founded it, and He will establish it forever. It is built upon a solid Rock. Make no mistake: the church is here to stay and what little appreciation and praise God receives from this world is through the body of Christ. Let us not give up meeting together, offering our humble worship, sacrifice, and service. In our thankfulness, let us be led to celebrate our Lord together.

When you are weary and when you are wary, walk around and notice the glory of God in this world and in your life. Make note of everything that stands firm and all that is beautiful. If God is your God, He will be your God forever. He will guide you and lead you purposefully through your life. You have been called up to that same mountain of holiness, so do not give up meeting together in fellowship with your brothers and sisters in Christ, especially when life becomes chaotic.

Lord, both rich and poor must hear the Word of God and respond, and those who forget You have no hope of rescue. I know the vanity of this world is insufficient to make me happy, and happy is the heart in which You are celebrated and honored. Help me remember how much You love and favor me, and direct my heart to serve You and Your people in the church and beyond.

> **The church, the people of Christ, will find a deeper reality only found in Jesus. And Jesus is always relevant in any culture and in any context.**

Restoration

Cleanse me with hyssop, and I will be clean;
    wash me, and I will be whiter than snow.
Let me hear joy and gladness;
    let the bones you have crushed rejoice.
Hide your face from my sins
    and blot out all my iniquity.

Create in me a pure heart, O God,
    and renew a steadfast spirit within me.
—*Psalm 51:7–10*

Read Psalms 51–54

In Psalms 52–54, we encounter psalms that echo the familiar sentiments we often hear from David. He had criticized those who did not follow God, ignored and rejected God, and caused harm to His faithful followers. He cried out for rescue and for God's justice to be poured out upon his enemies. He exhorted others to follow God completely and with pure hearts. But in Psalm 51 we encounter a very different situation.

David wrote this psalm after he had done something very wrong. He had committed adultery with Bathsheba when her husband, Uriah, was away in the army and she became pregnant. Originally planning to make sure Uriah believed the baby in Bathsheba's womb was his own, instead King David sent Uriah into an area of heavy battle fully knowing it was likely he would be killed, and he was. David then took Bathsheba to be his wife. Nathan, a prophet, confronted David about his wrongdoing. At first, David dismissed his admonition and was unapologetic. It wasn't long, however, before his guilt began to weigh on him and he wrote Psalm 51, revealing the agony of a soul truly twisted and conflicted by sin.

He acknowledged the wrong he had done against Uriah and the sin he'd committed against God's laws. His rebellious spirit was now broken. David began to look at the long list of his transgressions against God, knowing how they condemned him. He pleaded with God for his whole account to be completely erased from God's memory, but also from his own conscience. He wanted God to blot out the full picture so it couldn't be seen anymore. His guilt had stopped his joy, and he missed his Lord and longed most of all for the restoration of their relationship. He had sinned greatly. Murder, adultery, covering up of his sin, and his rigid resistance against repentance. It took a bold confrontation from Nathan to break through his unyielding heart, but once shaken, David came clean before God with complete honesty. In humble brokenness, he laid it all on the table and asked God to create in him a new, pure heart and renew a steadfast spirit within him.

Have you been living in rebellion against God, but know it's time to finally come clean? Have you been carrying around heavy guilt for the wrong you have committed in your life, not believing God can or will forgive you, let alone restore you? God simply wants you to be sorry when you sin against Him. It's time to lay it all out on the table and let God forgive you. Let him take your sin and blot it out of His mind and lift that weight from your conscience forever. Like the hyssop the Hebrews used to paint the blood on their doors that God's judgment might pass over them, let the blood of Jesus wash you whiter than snow.

Lord, disobedience and doing wrong things is what fallen people do in this fallen world. But then there is what You do. You wash us clean, forget what we have done, and You hide Your face from our sins forever. I praise You and thank You. Only You can create a new heart within me. Lord, make me a new person altogether.

Have you blown it? Big-time? Unfortunately, it's a fallen person's specialty. Blessedly, God's specialty is washing us clean and totally forgetting what we have done.

Betrayal and Deliverance

God, who is enthroned from of old,
   who does not change—
he will hear them and humble them,
   because they have no fear of God.

My companion attacks his friends;
   he violates his covenant.
His talk is smooth as butter,
   yet war is in his heart;
his words are more soothing than oil,
   yet they are drawn swords.
—*Psalm 55:19-21*

Have you ever been in a season where your true friends have been revealed? Even more, have you ever realized someone who you thought truly respected and cherished you, was just buttering you up for their own deceitful purposes? They betrayed you when you loved them, and all you ever wanted and wished for them was joy and success. David watched those he thought would stick by him when things got tough simply walk away from him. Not only walk away, but turn on him and seek his utter destruction. He found himself in the midst of "ravenous beasts," as he put it, "men whose teeth are spears and arrows" (57:4). People who were so free with their professions of respect and esteem but really had malice in their hearts. Their genteel approach was all part of a strategy. Smooth words were sharp swords. They would smile at his face, draw him in close for an embrace, and stab him right in the back. They broke every promise they'd made to him.

David endured this so many times he began to believe he couldn't trust anyone. However, David acknowledged that when many of his companions deserted him and turned on him, God raised up many new friends who became very loyal to him. He had found his dependable people, and most of all he realized who was always faithful, his Lord and Best Companion. The Judge who sits enthroned and has always presided over the affairs of men. David settled himself again to pray fervently morning, noon, and night and assured himself God would answer him in His timing. If not in victory, He would deliver David in patience, inward peace, and holy joy.

In the same way, trust your Best Companion, for Jesus completely understands what it's like to be rejected by people He loves desperately. Cast all your burdens on Him by faithful prayer. Be thankful for the blessings He has bestowed upon you, and whatever you still desire, leave it to Him to give it to you in His own way and timing. In the meantime, especially while you're healing, commit your life and works to Him and you will find yourself satisfied.

Lord, the biggest and most painful disappointments in this life are when those I love reject me and turn to me with heart-piercing malice. And I realize today that if eating three times a day can scarcely get me by, then praying three times a day must be a bare minimum. You are truly my best and most faithful Companion, and I often treat You with what must feel like such dismissive complacency. Please help me wrap my mind around the fact that You want nothing more than to sit down and listen to me talk to You about all my struggles.

Have you ever considered your burdens as gifts God has trusted you with for some loving and special purpose, one being that they may bring you closer to Himself? Therefore, cast your cares upon Him morning, noon, and night.

What God Allows

You have shown your people desperate times;
    you have given us wine that makes us stagger.
But for those who fear you, you have raised a banner
    to be unfurled against the bow.
—*Psalm 60:3-4*

A re you beginning to recognize the pattern of your own routine in the way David approached his life? He prayed. He complained about his troubles. He prayed again. He complained again. He declared his confidence in God. He prayed again. Then he sang.

David faced corrupt judges at the beginning of his troubles with King Saul. Judges who apparently were easily wooed by the King. They were learned men, well educated in the laws. They were men David had expected to be just and fair, not easily persuaded by bribes of greater power and financial security. Instead they used their own authority to plot with premeditation the unjust persecution of David. They held the balances of justice in their hands, but instead of doing what they ought, what was expected of them, they ruled in favor of tyranny and brutality. As those who are not in active service and submission to God, they were stubborn in their maliciousness and no words of reason would soften their hearts. As it is said, there are none so deaf as those who won't hear.

In these hard times and even in times of victory, we see David approach his enemies and his adversities the same. He was as devout in his prosperity as he was in his suffering. In Psalm 60, David reflected on the bad state of his people for many years, he noticed the blessed and happy turn of events for himself and his people as of late, he prayed for further deliverance from their enemies, and he asked God earnestly to keep carrying them, blessing them, and bringing them in perfect acquaintance with Him.

David struggled to understand the years he and his people had to contend with their own God, but he still found comfort in knowing God was the author of it all. When he felt as if God had cast him and his people off, he never stopped flying the banner of allegiance to Him. You can probably relate to David when you reflect on your seasons of ups and downs. If you are currently on a hill of respite and victory, be sure to look back and mark all the times you recognize God standing in the gap for you, protecting you, and leading you to greener pastures. Be grateful for your increased faith and wisdom as you march forward. If you are in a valley, take whatever comfort you can from knowing God is the Author of your life and He will not allow you to go through difficult circumstances or endure the cruel designs of your enemies without a loving purpose. Your confidence lies in believing the God of the universe is your God and any enemy of yours is an enemy of His. Read these psalms to foresee their future ruin and keep following David's pattern of prayer, believing, and singing.

Lord, help me understand these confusing times and circumstances of my life. Help me remember and cling with faith to Your promises of purposeful providence. To be honest, I can't see how any of this could ever really be good for me, but I will admit I have often mistaken Your blessed plans for awful burdens, only to be surprised and overjoyed again and again. I am praying hard and mustering all my strength to wave that banner of allegiance to You in the ever-changing winds of my life.

What God allows for the purposes of refining discipline, He restores in love and mercy.

Comfort in the Wilderness

Because your love is better than life,
    my lips will glorify you.
I will praise you as long as I live,
    and in your name I will lift up my hands.
I will be fully satisfied as with the richest of foods;
    with singing lips my mouth will praise you.
—*Psalm 63:3–5*

W e often find David truly crying out in his prayers to God. He wants to be heard. It's not enough for him to just vent his frustrations; he wants God to pay attention to him, to hear and listen, to take everything he's pouring out into consideration. He wants God's help and support in his times of distress, and he wants God to answer him quickly. David knows well not to place his confidence in the men of this world, no matter how close or how powerful. He knows not to place his confidence in his own power, authority, or wealth, which can be easily lost. David knows his only hope is in God.

David authored Psalm 63 when he was in the wilderness of Judah. He missed the communion he'd had with God in the temple, and he longed, in his banishment, for God's presence to be with him in the dry, desert wilderness. He acknowledged all the best things in this life; its best comforts and greatest abundance are no comparison to God's tenderness and consideration. It is within his spiritual life where he longed most to be fulfilled, and that is the place, his innermost self, where he found God's better provision. Within his fellowship with God, his longing and hunger are not simply maintained, but it is a nourished livelihood, rich and delicious. In all of David's hopes for personal restoration and delivery from the wilderness, none were greater than his hope for his close friendship and connection with his God to be fully mended. He settled himself to praise God at every thought of Him. He sought God's will in every decision and every direction. He did not want to be where God didn't want him, and if God wanted him in the desert wilderness, he was content to be there as long as God's presence and loving-kindness were with him.

There will likely be times when God will lead you to the wilderness. You will most assuredly feel lost, confused, and lonely as you wander the parched and desolate landscape. You will feel unsettled and quite at a loss as to what to do with yourself, but you must not let the hot and dry air get the best of you. Cry out to your God knowing you have the audience of a God who really exists and is ever-present. When you can't see anything even on the faraway horizon, seek God's favor and glory. Seek a deeper relationship with Him through His Word and seek a greater mercy from Him through prayer. Turn your focus to your spiritual life, which is eternal, rather than your physical life, which is temporary. Make all the days of your life thanksgiving days, even days lost in the wilderness. Remember all the delights of the world pale in comparison to living a life in service to God, being wholly fulfilled in your close friendship with Him, and resting in His favor.

Lord, hear my cry and listen to my prayer! I feel so lost sometimes and just can't figure out what to do or how to fix this vast and fruitless desert season. I want things to go back to the way they used to be or just get better somehow. I'm tired of wandering and I'm tired of feeling as if years are passing and I'm being left behind and missing out. I will resolve myself to stay here if that is Your will for me, but only if You will please be with me and let Your presence and favor be fully known to my heart.

Do you find yourself in dry seasons, wandering through a fruitless wilderness? In those times, your oasis is found in the Word, a thankful and giving spirit, and a closer prayer walk with Jesus.

An Ear to the Ground

You care for the land and water it;
    you enrich it abundantly.
The streams of God are filled with water
    to provide the people with grain,
    for so you have ordained it.
You drench its furrows and level its ridges;
    you soften it with showers and bless its crops.
You crown the year with your bounty,
    and your carts overflow with abundance.
—Psalm 65:9–11

G ood gardeners, by nature, are nurturing and caring souls. They tend to have a heart for wildlife and have a sense of time tuned in to nature. They have an ear to the ground, noting the pulse of the season; are acutely aware of winds of change; and have a mastery understanding of weather. They till up the hard earth and scatter and sow seeds in the softened soil. They are thrilled by the returning spring rains inundating the land and flooding fresh furrows. Good gardeners are constant, persistent, and patient, as there are decisions to be made every day regarding the health and future of their gardens. They are in the garden on a regular basis, making sure their plants get the care they require, catching problems and pests before they get out of hand. Good gardeners are exceptional observers and carefully watch for signs of change and distress. They keep a careful eye and tend to their gardens as they grow, pruning and pulling weeds as needed. Good gardeners pay attention to the climate, as they know what kind of weather makes a plant miserable or helps it adjust, protecting the plant before it wilts and rots in the soil. Good gardeners have artistic vision and creative expectation and are able to picture the end result of their careful and diligent work. They take great delight in their abundant harvest and share with everyone around them.

That God began His creative work on humankind in a garden may not be coincidence. God is your Good Gardener. He has an ear to the ground, noting the pulse of the season you are in. He's acutely aware of the winds of change in the ominous weather you are facing and that was predicted in your forecast. He's going to command the rains to fall, saturating and permeating every inch of your life. He's going to till and break up your rough spots, cultivating your heart to make it ready for new seed. He's going to keep pruning and weeding. He's going to pay attention to your climate, and He might move you into His greenhouse if He sees problems and pests He knows will bring you distress and make you unhappy. He's going to be constant, persistent, and patient knowing there are decisions to make over you every day regarding your health and future. Rest assured, your God has in mind for you an artistic vision and creative expectation. Even more than He does for the heavens and the earth. He knows and can see the picture of your end result. Your Father takes great delight in the abundant harvest He produces throughout your life, for your good and His glory, and His desire is for your vats to be so overflowing you are eager to share your fruit and bountiful testimony with others.

Lord, help me to think of my life as a garden. Help me remember, as part of Your creation, I am in need of Your constant attention. Your persistent seasons of plowing, cultivating, and drenching are purposeful, and Your constant poking around, picking at, and transplanting are best for my health. I started out as a little seedling in Your greenhouse, but You have a grand vision for my future. Remind my heart that all of this is about helping me grow strong that I may produce good fruit for Your kingdom. Lord, take my little mustard seed of faith today and grow it into an enormous tree with many branches.

Are you being pruned, drenched, or plowed? Rejoice! It's all part of the Good Gardener's visionary design.

Enduring with the Lord's Help

Hasten, O God, to save me;
    come quickly, LORD, to help me.

May those who want to take my life
    be put to shame and confusion;
may all who desire my ruin
    be turned back in disgrace.
—Psalm 70:1–2

Read Psalms 69-71

David's psalms are a continual returning to urgent petitions. He asks God to hear him, to listen to him, to save him, and to be with him. He is often very desperate for deliverance. If not deliverance, then to know and sense God's presence is with him. If not to save him, then to please, please give him strength so that he does not faint and lose heart altogether. David complains about his enemies again. They seek his body, to see him weary in pain and suffering. They seek his life, to see it in ruin, destruction, and even death. They seek his soul, to torment him and disturb his mind. They are cruel and devious, and attempt to convince him to give up on God, to turn to immoral and wicked ways to save himself.

Though David was indeed impoverished and unable to make ends meet, he cried out to God for help, maybe through teeth clenched tightly. He knew God was his only hope. He reminded God of the many times He had rescued him before. In so doing, he was also reminding himself. He begged God for rescue, but in the meantime, he begged God to just be with him, to give him strength to hold on, and that God would do so quickly. His grip on God surely slipped from time to time while being tossed to and fro.

If you are not facing physical enemies, you are surely facing spiritual enemies. Again, it is helpful to remember, especially when you find yourself in the wilderness, you have a very real Enemy who seeks to destroy. He is ever prowling around, searching for those he can devour. He seeks your body, to see it in pain and suffering. He seeks your life, to see it in ruin, pushing for physical and spiritual death. He seeks your soul, to torment you and to disturb your mind. He is cruel, utterly evil, and devious, and wants nothing more than to tempt you to turn away from God and turn to the world for your answers, or even more, to just give up and give in to sin.

David admitted he was desperately poor and needy. Reminding God of all the times He had come through for David in the past, honored Him. These are the words and the pleas of a person of faith. If you are spiritually destitute and having a hard time making ends meet, believe it or not, you are in a very good place. Take your prayers to a God with infinite mercy, who does not despise the heavy sighs of a broken heart. On the contrary, he has pronounced His blessing over those who are poor in spirit, and joy can be found in the simple pursuit, as God is a Rewarder of those who diligently seek Him. And if searching for God and praising Him becomes your continual habit, God will be magnified.

Lord, when I meditate upon all the times You have blessed me and rescued me just in the nick of time, I am girded up in my faith knowing You have been so faithful. I am also reminded not to get secure in myself or my circumstances, but to stay close to You. Thunderstorms and tornadoes are seasonal. They'll likely be coming around again. If You choose not to remove me from the path of these storms, please walk with me through them that I might not faint and be swallowed whole.

Are you lost and God is nowhere in sight? How much time have you spent looking for Him? Maybe it's time to double down and press in further until you find Him.

Do Not Be Fooled

Surely God is good to Israel,
　　to those who are pure in heart.

But as for me, my feet had almost slipped;
　　I had nearly lost my foothold.
For I envied the arrogant
　　when I saw the prosperity of the wicked.
—*Psalm 73:1–3*

A re you ever tempted to doubt if this whole Christian life is worth all the trouble? Especially when you see foolish people making foolish decisions and yet they come to no harm, prosper, and keep prospering? You, on the other hand, sift every decision carefully through the Word and in humble prayer. You respond to conviction and repent earnestly. You strive to live your life in a way pleasing to God, yet still find yourself in dry deserts of testing. You step out of line just a little and find yourself quickly lost in a harsh wasteland of reproof. You wander through the wilderness, wondering where God is, crying out for mercy and deliverance, but He seems far-off and silent. His presence is felt only in His persistent pruning and weeding. His voice is heard only when He says, "No," or "Not yet."

Meanwhile, the ungodly seem to have some sort of inexplicable exemption or special privilege ensuring them very little trouble in life. Not only are they rich, they increase in riches. They thrive and abound in honor, power, money, and pleasure while others work hard for everything they have. The author in Psalm 73 was also tempted to question the benefit of duty and devotion, until he realized those who live a life full of easy wealth and pleasure often think very highly of themselves. All their success doesn't really do them, or anyone else, any good. They have no fear of God, nor do they desire to know or submit to Him. Why should they? They begin to think, if there is a God, they must somehow be above Him. They are unaware He is watching and taking account of everything they say, think, and do. They are dismissive of a heavenly Father who would gladly show them how to use all He had given them wisely, for their good and His glory.

Right off the bat, the psalmist reminded himself that God is faithful to those who are pure in heart. Those who are washed in the blood of Christ and robed in His righteousness. Those who are cleansed through willing repentance and a divine renewing of the mind. Though we may not always understand why God, who has and gives everything, is so free with His blessing to so many, we must believe He knows what He is doing and acknowledge He has the authority to do as He pleases. We must resolve and accept that there is a transcendent goodness and fairness about God and have faith that all He does is meaningful and loving. Therefore, we do not follow, submit, and sacrifice in vain. Though we might be tempted to think there is nothing to profit in this battle that is the Christian life, when it's all said and done, "Blessed are the pure in heart, for they will see God" (Matthew 5:8).

Lord, I admit I have wondered from time to time if this Christian life, this life of refining and sanctifying, is worth all the trouble. Especially when I see others having such an easy go of things. Especially when you call me to sacrifice or submit in areas I don't see You calling others to, not even fellow believers. It often seems it would make my life a whole lot easier to let those callings go by the wayside. I know and believe I am not following You in vain, but Lord, help me in my unbelief.

There is no harm in being successful and having wealth. It is when we become proud, boastful, and self-assured that it ceases to be blessing and becomes a glittering but weighty curse.

God Is Still on His Throne

You say, "I choose the appointed time;
    it is I who judge with equity.
When the earth and all its people quake,
    it is I who hold its pillars firm."
—*Psalm 75:2-3*

Read Psalms 75-77

D o you get discouraged and feel hopeless when you turn on the news or browse social media? It doesn't take long to be reminded we are a hurting people living in a hurting world. Asaph is described as a contemplative, believing man, but a hint of sorrow washes over his psalms. He lives in a time of much disunity. Nations rise against nations. Friction and controversy divide people into opposing factions. Dishonesty and bad behavior among the parties completely dissolve nations and their people. If Asaph can't find integrity and righteousness around him, he ransacks the past for reminders of the victories and glories of God. God Himself speaks to remind him He is still on his throne.

Leaders among people should remember they are assigned posts of service. The citizenry hopes they will lead with integrity and by the rules of justice. However, even when they fail to do so, God reminds us He is the Judge. His throne is never vacant, nor has He resigned or retired from His authority. By some awesome and divine design, God is using the leaders of this world for His heavenly purposes. This truth can be hard to understand and accept when we witness so much strife and division, but just as Jesus came, saving the whole world from the utter ruin of sin, God's providential purposes are the shoulders carrying the whole world.

As much as we can be assured that God is ever on His throne, so too can we believe He is never early or late. Just as He set the sun, moon, and stars on their course and the seasons on their cycle, He has set and appointed the times of man. He has determined the time when He will intercede and say, "No more," and when that time comes, His intervention will be swift and certain. When nations rise and are prosperous, but forget it is God who has blessed them for His purposes, He has a way of humbling them. When lawlessness is everywhere and tyrants from all factions are in power, it threatens the stability of all things. When the earthly mountains of authority begin to crumble, we can be assured God upholds and sustains the righteous. Jesus gives us the counsel, "do not lift your horns against heaven" (75:5), boasting in our own prerogative. He calls us not to persist in our contempt of the government set over us, but to trust God is actively on His throne. Know the punishment of the wicked is already prepared, and God holds the cup Himself. Those who were unyielding and scoffed at His salvation and peace, and those who professed it, will one day be brought to the seat of judgment.

Lord, it can be easy for me to forget You are on Your throne when I look at this world of hurting and hopelessness. Help me remember my battle isn't against people, but the powers of deception. Thank You for the promise that You are still on Your throne and You will, on that appointed day, come and make all things right. Supply me with a heart of empathy and love for those who tread over Your Word and Your people as each day You, Yourself, wait patiently for them to accept Your salvation gift, not wanting anyone to perish.

God is on His throne. Are there areas in your own life where this truth and reminder needs to be applied?

History Reveals the Hand of God

In spite of all this, they kept on sinning;
in spite of his wonders, they did not believe.
So he ended their days in futility
and their years in terror. . . .

Yet he was merciful;
he forgave their iniquities
and did not destroy them.
Time after time he restrained his anger
and did not stir up his full wrath.
He remembered that they were but flesh,
a passing breeze that does not return.
—*Psalm 78:32-33; 38-39*

Read Psalm 78

P salm 78 is a review of important events in Israel's history and the longest historical psalm. It's intended to be viewed as a parable, that it will be a lesson for generations to follow, a song that it might be better remembered. It's a narrative of the powerful miracles God displayed and the great mercies He showered over His children. It's a chronicle of the heavy sins that provoked Him and the evidence of God's displeasure and anger they had suffered because of their sins.

God had done so many miraculous things to rescue and bless the Israelites, from Moses all the way to David. In fact, it seems there was nothing He wouldn't do for His children. There shouldn't have been any question in their minds about God's power and His willingness to use it for their benefit. The Lord had delivered them from the oppressions of Egypt, parted a mighty sea, given them manna, water, meat, and much more, and yet they still grumbled, doubted, and complained. God was infuriated with His children because He loved them. He had proved Himself many times over, so it broke His heart that they still doubted His willingness and ability to deliver and bless them. It was never long before they would reveal their discontent and unbelieving hearts. They always wanted more, and soon they cared only about the lusts of their own hearts to be satisfied rather than to honor and obey the mighty and loving God who had brought them into prosperity. "So he ended their days in futility."

This is a warning so that history might not again repeat itself, that the children of God must not be unbelieving. To question God's power is to speak against Him in the same way we see the Israelites doing. We must take care not to persist in our unwavering unbelief, as it seems nothing grieves our Father more than being hopeless in His ability and faithless in His love for us, especially when He has never failed His children. Our takeaway from this historical song of remembrance and teaching is that God is worthy of our adoration, and gratitude for His wondrous works, miracles, strength, and greatness is far and above all. History surely reveals the hand of God moving throughout the people and times of this world, the goodness and kindness of God to His stubborn and rebellious people. This psalm is assuredly honest about the many failings of His people in the past and undoubtedly a mirror where we can sadly see ourselves in many ways. Our saving grace is found in the boundless mercy and persistent patience we observe in the Lord throughout time.

Lord, I praise and thank You for Your Word and its guiding instruction revealing Your unfolding faithful story. I know it is Your desire that I learn from the mistakes of those who came before me, rather than learn through affliction. May I daily return to affirm my hope in You, to learn to trust in You for all things, and to be encouraged to obey and keep Your commandments, that my days might not end in futility. Not only for my benefit, but that I will be prepared and equipped to share this testimony with the younger generation after me.

Take care not to forget the works God has already accomplished for you. Pore over the remembrances in His Word to help avoid the errors of previous generations.

Make a Joyful Noise

> Sing for joy to God our strength;
>> shout aloud to the God of Jacob!
> Begin the music, strike the timbrel,
>> play the melodious harp and lyre.
>
> Sound the ram's horn at the New Moon,
>> and when the moon is full, on the day of our
>>> festival;
> this is a decree for Israel,
>> an ordinance of the God of Jacob.
> —*Psalm 81:1-4*

F rancis Scott Key was the lawyer, author, and poet who wrote "The Star-Spangled Banner."[6] In a similar way, so too was Asaph a national songster. His specialty was repeating and reciting the history of his country in prayerful and patriotic psalmody. In Psalm 79 he sang of a city in ruin, a time of invasion, oppression, and national overthrow. In Psalm 80 he composed another lamentation of national woe, a mournful testimony of the church as a lily among thorns. Psalm 81 begins as a song of praise to celebrate a memorable day in Israel's history, ending with a picture of their happiness had they only been faithful to their God. These national anthems may have spoken to the Israelites in the Old Testament, but have been written by divine inspiration and purpose for our own learning and application all these generations later.

Just as God appointed feast days for the Israelites to celebrate and reverently remember all He had done for them, He has also appointed days for us to do the same. God's callings for his children to keep meeting together and honor the Sabbath day are the same in that they call us to come together to praise God for who He is and what He has done for us. We are the bride of Christ and must be willing to gently but earnestly admonish one another when we see a brother or sister slipping away into danger, reminding them of the protection and happiness they will have if they will but remain in God.

God is always available to meet with us wherever we are, but He has appointed His solemn days for His followers to gather together. They are to gather together in the spirit of fellowship, serving and encouraging one another, as there is work to be done. We do not go to church to be idle and sluggish, but to become excited about the work the Lord has for us to do within the church and out in the world. We also gather together to collectively give the glory and praise due His name. We must do this in the same way the nation of Israel came together to remember and honor the Lord at their appointed feasts. We must do this with the same grateful loyalty as when our flag is waving majestically and we're collectively singing our national anthem. When the bride of Christ gathers in this way, it is a reflection of heaven.

Has attending church simply become a weekly ritual? Is it easy to skip altogether when life gets busy? Has the true purpose of honoring God's appointed day become lost and convoluted somehow?

Lord, thank You for opening my eyes through the many examples in Your historical testimony. I can clearly see the truth and edifying purpose of Your mandates. Jesus, You are the strength of every believer. With Your help, I am able to endure all my sufferings and have enough left over to serve You and the people around me. Because of this, may I rush to Your appointed day to worship You with a joyful noise.

God is to be worshiped with joy and reverence. We must rise and praise Him proudly, as those who are not ashamed of our dependence on Him or our duties and responsibilities to Him.

Strength Found in Praise and Worship

Blessed are those whose strength is in you,
    whose hearts are set on pilgrimage.
As they pass through the Valley of Baka,
    they make it a place of springs;
    the autumn rains also cover it with pools.
They go from strength to strength,
    till each appears before God in Zion.
—*Psalm 84:5-7*

Read Psalms 82-84

In Psalm 82 we see Asaph, the patriotic poet, reproving leaders who sold themselves in bribery to those who oppressed the poor and needy. He complained knowing they would not receive good and virtuous instruction. Though they saw the world in confusion and turmoil, they forgot and dismissed that it was their appointed duty to act justly. God had not stepped away as Supreme Ruler, and when leaders stepped away from His prerogatives, did not submit to His authority, and confused right and wrong, Asaph asked God to restore to order what had been tossed into uncertainty and confusion. Psalm 83 was Asaph's last song. He sang again of wars and dangers. He could see peril up ahead, but his focus was entirely upon God. He didn't ask for a brave leader or a mighty human force, but cast all his burdens and worries upon the Lord. Asaph was confident in God's ability to recover and restore His rightful dominion over the situation. The allied forces threatening his people broke up their partnership, which led to a mutual slaughter. They set out to destroy Israel together, but instead destroyed each other.

We return to a song of David in Psalm 84. He longed for the communion of the temple, recalled how blessed those were who were dwelling inside, and prayed earnestly to be able to return quickly. This is another psalm speaking to the importance and privilege of meeting together in worship and fellowship, attending Sabbath days and solemn assemblies. David, without this fellowship, realized even more how essential and worthy it was to him. He was even jealous of the birds who nested near the temple. David didn't want to just observe the ceremonies, but desired to offer his sacrifice of praise, lean his whole heart into God, and make progress in his faith.

Nothing, not even tyrant leaders, approaching danger, deserts, or wilderness will prevent those who love and trust God from making a pilgrimage to Him and His sanctuary. Nothing is more desirable than to worship God, and nothing can prevent them, even if their way should be through dry and barren wastelands. They submit to the inconvenience, holding precious the blessing and freedom of hearing the gospel. They leave the comfort and ease of their nests, forgoing their own convenience, allowing nothing to interfere, rather than profess themselves to be servants of God so long as there is no sacrifice or exertion required. David and Asaph direct us to prayer, to submission, and to the sanctuary of praise and worship, not only when our paths are cheerful and easy, but when we must walk through dry places as well.

Lord, help me remember when I am most over-whelmed, when it seems most difficult to carve out time for You, is the exact time when I need You the most. Please show me the things in my life that may be superfluous, things I can give up, to meet with You. When I am overloaded with responsibil-ities I can't cut away, please stretch my time, my strength, and my will, that I may not be persuaded to neglect You.

Some give themselves over to sleep, plea-sure, or gain when they hear the church bells ringing. Let not the comfort of your own nest keep you from praising God and hearing the Word preached in His house.

Winter Can Be Deceiving

Love and faithfulness meet together;
   righteousness and peace kiss each other.
Faithfulness springs forth from the earth,
   and righteousness looks down from heaven.
The LORD will indeed give what is good,
   and our land will yield its harvest.
Righteousness goes before him
   and prepares the way for his steps.
—Psalm 85:10–13

H ave you ever found yourself in unimaginable, unbearable circumstances? Seasons that have caused you extreme sorrow and grief? Have you ever felt confused because you love God and try your best to follow Him faithfully? Why has He then allowed such a heartbreaking and seemingly unfair thing to happen to you? As we squint our eyes and peer deeper into the Psalms, we begin to see more clearly. We see David singing of former mercies and begging God to remember him. He challenged God, pleaded his case, and desperately questioned God's motives, but then he quieted himself and decided to listen to God. He set his heart on what he knew to be true about his Father and his Father's promises. He resolved to put his hope in God.

We observe how the seasons of the earth both bless and afflict. Summer brings warmth and bounty, and autumn brings a harvest. Winter turns everything cold. Living things freeze and sometimes they die, but spring comes again. Life sprouts upward with buds, then blooms into full blossoms. As followers of Christ, we might wonder why we are not spared from the reaping and cutting seasons and the deadness of winter. Jesus has assured us there will be trouble in this life, even for God's children. The promise wasn't that we would be spared, though we often are. The promise was and is that we will be sustained, carried, and embraced.

Surely God will speak peace to His people. Mercy and truth shall meet together. The faithful look up to Jesus, and He looks down with mercy. Righteousness and peace kiss each other. God bestows spiritual blessings as well as material provisions of comfort. Just a taste, but not an overindulgence. While God may grant to His beloved a season of abundance, He does not stuff our bellies as He calls us to look upward to higher and more important possessions.

However, when the unbearable happens, have you found comfort in bitterness instead? Since your leaves have all been cut back, have you attempted to cover yourself up in anger to keep warm? Take heart today, as winter can be deceiving. You might not be growing, but you're still hanging on. You may be dormant, but God has not forgotten you. This is how you become resistant to the cold. Evergreens have been well prepared for the stress of these bone-chilling seasons, and miraculously, hope sprouts and buds in suffering and faith blooms in sorrow.

Lord, my heart is completely encased in winter. What I never wanted to happen has happened. What now? How do I survive this unwelcome, inhospitable, freezing-cold space in time? To be honest, I don't think I have anything left in me, no part of me that wants to survive. I need Your help! Lord, I am crying out from this raw and biting arctic! Please shine Your light and life upon me, that the hope and faith, lying icy and dormant within me, may somehow bud and blossom again.

When the lily of the valley blooms, happiness is said to return. Be brave enough to hold your hand out to your Savior until sweetness and happiness return to your valley again.

Gird Up Your Faith

I will sing of the Lord's great love forever;
   with my mouth I will make your faithfulness
      known
   through all generations.
I will declare that your love stands firm forever,
   that you have established your faithfulness in
      heaven itself.
—*Psalm 89:1–2*

P salm 89 was written by Ethan the Ezrahite, a musician during David's reign, and revered for his wisdom during Solomon's day. Solomon, King David's son, became king after David's death. During King Solomon's reign, his people prospered. Troubles began toward the end of his reign when he began to marry hundreds of foreign women. These new wives brought with them the worship of their false gods and turned Solomon's head and heart toward these pagan deities. His tolerance toward these false gods spread to the people of Israel. God was angry and split the country in two. After King Solomon died, his son Rehoboam became king. He made the decision to rule over his people with a heavy hand, and many turned away from him and made Jeroboam their king. Throughout the years these two kings would fight against each other. Sometimes Rehoboam would win, and sometimes Jeroboam would be victorious. Rehoboam continued the practice of setting up altars and shrines to worship false gods. The people began to engage in practices that greatly displeased God. Eventually, the Israelites came under Egyptian rule as punishment. Rehoboam's reign lasted only seventeen years.

Ethan must have written this psalm in his old age, as he lived long enough to know God's covenant with David and the prosperity of Solomon, and now witnessed the society crumbling under Rehoboam. He began by reminding and reaffirming himself of God's covenant promise to the house of David and encouraged the loyal people of God to gird up their faith against the daunting and dangerous temptations now surrounding them. What Ethan observed in these troubling times might have caused him to conclude God had rescinded His promise. Nevertheless, he resolved to praise God forever and he began to go over the terms of the contract. He realized it was God who maintained His commitment to David's line of descent, even when the leaders and the citizens strayed and were outright unfaithful to Him. Ethan, standing amid the ruins of his people, proceeded to mournfully pour out his petitions. He closed with a double invocation of blessing, "Amen and Amen" (v. 52).

Are you looking around convinced none of what you are seeing in this world can be saved or redeemed? It's simply too far gone. Are you standing amid the ruins of your life, convinced God has forgotten or rescinded His promises to you personally? Draw up hope from the deep well of these verses. God's mercy and truth stand eternally firm, not moved by any person. His justice and mercy will stand, one on each side of you. Not because you never stray, but because your God is always faithful.

Lord, I am very grateful for the assurances in this psalm. You have appointed Your reign on earth, and those who forsake Your laws will surely be punished with the rod. While nations rise and fall, Your design and plan will not be hindered. And I'm sure to be tested and strengthened in the wilderness and disciplined and refined in the desert, You will never betray Your faithfulness to me or Your steadfast people.

It has been said that a God who is all merciful would be unjust; but a God of all justice without mercy would be terrible indeed. Rejoice! Once and for all He has sworn His covenant salvation promise.

Divine Protection

Whoever dwells in the shelter of the Most High
    will rest in the shadow of the Almighty.
I will say of the LORD, "He is my refuge and my
       fortress,
    my God, in whom I trust." . . .

"Because he loves me," says the LORD, "I will rescue
       him;
    I will protect him, for he acknowledges my name.
He will call on me, and I will answer him;
    I will be with him in trouble,
    I will deliver him and honor him."
—*Psalm 91:1–2; 14–15*

D oes it seem as though nothing ever works out the way you want? Are your plans constantly thwarted? Are all your attempts foiled? Are people always failing and disappointing you? Psalm 90 was written by Moses and is the oldest of the psalms. We know that Abraham and his people were sojourners in exile. They were homeless strangers never finding permanent shelter, calm, or relief. They drifted from place to place in the land of Canaan until they finally made their way to Egypt. If the people had hopes of security and refuge in Egypt, they were soon dashed, as they were still barely tolerated. It was necessary for these wandering fugitives to find refuge in the shadow of their God, a dwelling place where the Lord sustained them under His wing.

Psalm 91 speaks again of the safety and security of those who hide themselves in the shadow of the Almighty. Psalm 92 is a Sabbath song reminding us to find rest, not in idleness, but in the meditation and celebration in God's greatness and power. Psalm 93 tells us that when we forget to place our confidence and hope in the power of God, we strip and rob God of His authority in our lives. We will not be sure of anything if we're not sure of God's sovereign control.

Do you place your faith in your own strength and find yourself running the same race over and over, yet never gaining any ground? Do you place your expectations in others, hoping they will bring you satisfaction, peace, and happiness, but always find yourself disappointed? Do you profess in word that God reigns, but not believe or feel God's power is truly available to you? Have all these unmet expectations left you feeling discouraged and frustrated?

Your encouragement is found in Moses as he considered the frailty of humankind, humbled himself to God's plan for himself and his people, and committed himself to pray for divine mercy and for God's favor to shine upon them. Abraham, Moses, and the people of God have always traveled this world as vagabonds, but if you sincerely resolve to submit to God as your Keeper, you will be taken under the mysterious and exceptional care of your Lord. You will experience the invincible power and support of God against all challenges and temptations. You will find satisfaction, peace, and happiness in Jesus Christ, freeing yourself and others from meeting that unattainable expectation. You will find safe haven and divine protection from rough waters in the harbor of God. You will run a meaningful race, gaining ground, until you run straight through the door of your permanent home already prepared for you in heaven.

Lord, I often seek out numerous hiding places all in vain. The fundamental truth is that You reign. You have established the world and Your throne. May I not only confess this with my mouth, but believe it in my heart, that I am the object of Your special love and goodness. If I keep You as the focus of my expectations and hope, You will be my invincible shield and I will gain meaningful ground.

This whole life is a temporary journey. The tent of God is your portable shelter, supported by sturdy poles, durable fabric stretched tight by indestructible cords attached to secure pegs driven deep into the ground.

Sanctified Affliction

Blessed is the one you discipline, Lᴏʀᴅ,
    the one you teach from your law;
you grant them relief from days of trouble,
    till a pit is dug for the wicked.
For the Lᴏʀᴅ will not reject his people;
    he will never forsake his inheritance.
—*Psalm 94:12–14*

T he founding fathers of our nation set out to establish a republic where people would be free to worship and practice their religion without the infringement of the government. The government was to protect this freedom. Today it seems as if the opposite is true. Many people, along with our own government, are intent on prohibiting the free practice, worship, and service of Christianity. For example, movements to prohibit Christian groups from distributing Bibles are on the rise as well as campaigns to prohibit Christian businesses from making choices based on their conscience and religious belief. Crusades have been set in place to ban Christian expression and drive Christian groups and Christian businesses from college campuses. However, secularism, evolutionism, and humanism not only go unchecked, but are freely promoted and broadcasted by the government, especially within the education system. Our leadership is much more inclined to persecute the religious of this day than to protect them.

The author of Psalm 94 is not known, but many scholars are confident this is another psalm of David. This author also lived in a time when his own society and government began to heartily proclaim and spread depravity and persecute righteousness. The wicked of the day pursued their own interests for their own gain to the detriment of those in society most vulnerable, and the government had become their ally. The corrupt seemed to have succeeded as they overcame virtue, morality, and integrity. They even convinced themselves of their superiority, foolishly thinking the Lord did not see what they did, and if He did, He didn't care.

The author made his plea to the Supreme Judge, mentioning the God of vengeance twice. He believed God alone was able to turn the spiritual and moral tide because it was God's spoken responsibility to do so. He spoke to those who made these ridiculous claims of God's complacency, calling them senseless fools, and he appealed to them to repent. He then spoke to the still faithful, giving them words of comfort. He reminded them that God used wicked men and their oppression as a vital part of their sanctification. He ended by rehearsing the promises of protection and deliverance of God's own. Not only do we have His salvation promise and sustaining grace in the midst of adversity, we also have the assurance that when the time comes, the wicked will be dealt with justly.

Psalms 95 and 96 form a pair, marching orders to the faithful to press on in the pursuit of God and His service. Because our Lord is the one and only great God, we should worship Him with joyful praise, never cease sharing the salvation message and testimonies of His faithfulness, and wait expectantly for His future arrival to one day judge the world.

Lord, I will admit that I often feel as if evil is winning. I sometimes wonder myself if You're watching and why You don't intervene. Though I know I shouldn't stop proclaiming Your truth, at best it's ignored or dismissed, at worst it brings condescension, mockery, and persecution. Remind me again and again of Your well-established plan and my mission to worship, witness, and wait.

Are you weary of being refined while the wicked seem to get a pass? Take heart, for it is better to endure the sanctification of affliction now than suffer the wrath of God against the boastful and unrepentant later.

Sing a New Song

Sing to the LORD a new song,
>   for he has done marvelous things;
his right hand and his holy arm
>   have worked salvation for him.
The LORD has made his salvation known
>   and revealed his righteousness to the nations.
—Psalm 98:1-2

Read Psalms 97–99

T hese three psalms celebrate the divine plan of the gospel, the coming kingdom of heaven, and the coronation of the conquering Messiah. The Lord reigns and His people will be elated when the whole world acknowledges Him. They are touched and lit up with the glory of God, they esteem and praise His name because God has made known to them His salvation, and they dread the just and righteous justice of those who reject His ordinances and saving help.

They sing to Him a new song for He has done wonderful things. Victory was won by His right hand and holy arm. He conquered and cleared all the obstacles that kept us from the finish line. The Enemy's fortress and strongholds have been crushed. Satan and all his loyal principalities have been disarmed and defeated. God sought out a people of His own and pursued us. He raised up His Son and Jesus came to accomplish the covenant promise of the Old Testament and His death victoriously nailed our death to the cross.

Time and time again we are called upon to express our joy and gratefulness and give God praise for who He is and what He has done. God's love and grace give the new believer a new heart in their chests and a new song in their mouths and in the new heaven and the new earth we will be given new songs to sing. If those who believed in the promise of the Messiah's first coming and rejoiced, we, who know it was finished on the cross, can celebrate the promise of His second coming. When that time comes, the whole earth and everything on it will welcome the new King to the throne with sacred songs. When once the fallen earth groaned with pain of brokenness, raging, crumbling, and shaking against us, it will now rise up with us in great happiness and delight. The sea will be filled with reverberating echoes of praise, the rivers will clap their hands in applause and adoration, and the mountains will all sing in joyful chorus.

Has it been a while since you've made a joyful noise? Have you been too busy or burdened? Perhaps you feel the seed of light God has sown in you has been choked out by weeds. Take heart; you will have a flame of God's glory if you love and serve Him. That light is eternal, and nothing can take it away from you because God has placed it there Himself. But maybe it's time you changed your tune. Let the glory of the Redeemer and the joy of the redeemed be ignited fresh in you today. Make a joyful noise! Rejoice and sing His praises, for He has done marvelous things, and marvelous things are still to come.

Lord, despite all that's going wrong in my life right now, I have so much more to be thankful for. Open my eyes more and more to see the bigger picture. You are the conquering Messiah over all time and nations. You crushed all my obstacles. Your mercies and blessings are new every morning. May I wake each day with a fresh trumpet blast of celebration, for there is so much to praise and applaud!

Sing to Him a new song. Change your mind and your attention. Sing a different tune as you welcome Him to the throne of your heart.

The Good Shepherd

Worship the LORD with gladness;
   come before him with joyful songs.
Know that the LORD is God.
   It is he who made us, and we are his;
   we are his people, the sheep of his pasture.
—*Psalm 100:2-3*

We come across another lament of an afflicted man in Psalm 102. Deep and pressing sorrow fills his complaints. Can you relate to his cries? Are your days passing like smoke? Are your bones on fire? Is your heart filled with canker and blight? Do all your prayers begin with begging Him to just hear you over and over because you doubt He's really listening? If He were, God would surely do something, but all you have to sustain you is dry ashes and bitter tears. Life used to be better, not perfect, but better than this! You don't understand what's happened. How did you get here? It's as if God has, after walking before you and leading you, just lifted you up and thrown you aside. Your whole life is lived in the shadow of evening and you can't escape. You're blocked in all around.

Adding insult to injury, Psalms 100 and 101 just encouraged you to shout for joy, to worship the Lord with gladness, to sing of His love and justice, to be careful, and to live a blameless life! You're trying, but this cloud of darkness has settled in around you. You can't see where you've gone wrong and you can't see your way out, let alone to your way to God. How are you supposed to come before the Lord with joyful songs if you can't see Him?

In the book of John, chapter 10, we read about many different flocks of sheep being gathered into a single pen for the night. The sheep have different shepherds and they get hopelessly mixed together during the night. The only way to the highlands is through the valley of testing and trial. Jesus is our Good Shepherd and He gives us careful scrutiny, using His rod to separate the wool from the skin. He checks for health and quality, and searches for thistles and burrs. His rod is for correction and His staff is for guidance. The Shepherd has gone before us to prepare the highlands for us, and He knows the way. He has assured us we can make it. He has counted the sheep of His flock carefully; not one will be lost in the mix. The Shepherd will come in the morning, preaching a message His sheep will follow, for they recognize His voice. You remember that the Lord is God. It is He who made you, and you are His. You are not lost in the mix, but a sheep of His benevolent, green pasture. When you can't see him through the darkness, perk your ears to hear the warmth of His voice. Your night may be filled with weeping, but joy will come in the morning.

Lord, my days are like the evening shadow; I wither away like grass. But you, O Lord, sit enthroned forever. You will arise and have compassion on me, for it is time to show me favor. You will respond to my bleating prayers and not leave me destitute. You will come for me in the morning and rebuild.

If the Lord has fenced you in for the night, be assured He will come for you in the morning. Your journey is far from over. One bright, sunny day, you will enter His gates with thanksgiving and His courts with praise.

All His Benefits

Praise the LORD, my soul;
    all my inmost being, praise his holy name.
Praise the LORD, my soul,
    and forget not all his benefits— . . .

Praise the LORD, my soul.

LORD my God, you are very great;
    you are clothed with splendor and majesty.
—*Psalms 103:1–2; 104:1*

David was the stated author of Psalm 103, and scholars believe he was also the author of Psalm 104. The first is a psalm filled with celebration of the goodness of God, His fatherly compassion, and tender mercies. The breadth and width of Psalm 104 celebrated His distinct greatness, divine majesty, artistic mastery, and His sovereign dominion over all. He gave God glory for the distinguished power of the heavens and as Creator and Master of the land and sea. He gave God glory for the precise provision given in the maintenance of all the creatures according to their specific nature and need. He gave God glory for the meticulous course of the sun and moon, days, nights, seasons, and all the carefully placed furnishings and appointments of the sea. He gave God glory for His ultimate and supreme power over all He has created.

In Psalm 103 we see a song bursting out in praise. It is thought that David wrote this psalm when he had the eyes of someone older and wiser, with much experience following his Shepherd through the peaks and valleys of his life. Even so, David still began his song by working himself up in worship. He strained his entire being—his heart, mind, soul, and strength—everything that was within him to attempt to express fully his feelings. He examined himself and still found reason to admonish himself for his apathy. He reminded himself again of all God's benefits, for the forgiveness of those who were heavily burdened by their sins and the physical and spiritual healing He brought to them. He remembered the redemption God extended, pulling us from the pit of destruction and the guilt of our disobedience and sin, crowning us with kindness and mercy. David declared the Lord satisfies our every desire with good things, renewing our youth.

Maybe you're still under a cloud of darkness. Think back to a time when the skies cleared and you emerged into the warmth of His light. Did you find yourself trying to pray, trying to sing at church, or in your car when a praise song began to play, but being so overwhelmed you began to choke on your words? Were you so overwhelmed as you stood in the presence of God's flooding and overflowing goodness that you could only weep out your joy and humble thanksgiving?

The Bible is full of encouragement urging us to remember and to forget not because we are absentminded creatures. Do you talk to yourself and remind yourself about God? How often do you contemplate the greatness of your Creator God, the God who has always proved Himself true, the God who has blanketed you with grace? How often do you meditate on His splendor and benevolent blessings?

Lord, though it might not be easy to do today, I come before You to praise Your Holy Name with my innermost being and with everything in me. I will remember who You are and everything You have already accomplished in the world and in my own life. I will muster my strength and place my hope in Your never-failing faithfulness. Please come quickly.

Those who walk with the Lord do not grow weary with age, but instead their youth is renewed. Though they may age on the outside, their innermost self is renewed day by day.

His Covenant Promises

Many times he delivered them,
>   but they were bent on rebellion
>   and they wasted away in their sin.
Yet he took note of their distress
>   when he heard their cry;
for their sake he remembered his covenant
>   and out of his great love he relented.
—Psalm 106:43–45

Read Psalms 105–106

T he author of these two psalms is not known for certain. Psalm 105 describes the journey of the Lord's people and His watchful care over them and His guidance of them from place to place. It opens with verses filled with praises and encouragement, for His people exalt their God. Psalm 106 is a counterpart to Psalm 105. Psalm 105 highlights God's grace in dealing with His people, and Psalm 106 also shines a spotlight on His grace, but against the dark backdrop of His people's repeated flagrant sins. After beginning with another call to praise God, the author began a long confession of the nation's sins during the exodus, the wandering in the wilderness, and when they entered the land of Canaan.

Though God displayed His great miracles right before their eyes, the people soon forgot His amazing works. They began to grumble and complain and move forward without seeking His counsel. Envy rose against Moses and Aaron, and at Horeb they made and worshiped a golden calf. After the report of the spies, not believing God's promise, they completely rejected the pleasant land God had for them. They yoked themselves to a false Moabite god and provoked the Lord to wrath at the waters of Meribah. They spared the nations God had doomed to destruction while convincing themselves they would not join them in their false ways, but it wasn't long before they mingled in their culture. At first it seemed harmless enough, but little by little they fell. They fell so far, in fact, that they adopted the custom of sacrificing their children to Molech, believing this false god would give them ease and blessing. The holy land was utterly polluted and no longer a comfort to them. It became an unfit place to receive God's blessings and He brought judgment upon them, or rather, they brought it upon themselves. With their defenses down their enemies made quick work of them, but even after all they had done, God took pity on them and remembered they were dust. He chose to forgive and restore them, not because of anything they had done, but because He is full of incomprehensible and tender mercy and eternally faithful to His covenant promises.

Israel's example shows us it is possible to witness great miracles and be the very focus of great mercies and still harden our hearts and forget God's overflowing kindness. They believed His promise, but only when they received it. Their faith was not a genuine saving faith that endured, but a superficial faith they forgot as soon as trials approached. When they groaned and complained in their cravings, God gave in to their requests, along with the consequences, and it made them sick in overindulgence. However, the more they dug themselves into great depths of sin, God's grace proved deeper still.

Lord, I praise and thank You for Your boundless grace. How often I forget You and fall into deep pits of sin. Give me a good memory so I might not forget how many times You have miraculously delivered me from the oppressive captivity of my own making and how many times You have provided abundant care and guidance while I wandered through the wilderness. Give me a heart of faith to follow You to the promised land.

As you look at and contemplate this long list of sins, examine yourself. Confess and repent of any you find hiding in your heart.

Righteous Indignation

Help me, Lord my God;
   save me according to your unfailing love.
Let them know that it is your hand,
   that you, Lord, have done it.
While they curse, may you bless;
   may those who attack me be put to shame,
   but may your servant rejoice.
—*Psalm 109:26–28*

Read Psalms 107-109

Psalm 107 reveals God's quick and well-timed rescue and care for His people and humankind in general. The psalmist rehearsed some of the most common misfortunes and hardships people suffer under in life. He spoke about banishment and scattering, captivity and imprisonment, sickness and torment, danger and distress. While this song can be sung at any recollection of physical and practical rescue, it mainly magnifies spiritual deliverance. The author closed with the encouragement that anyone who recollects and takes note of the works of the Lord will be filled with gratitude and praise. Psalm 108 is described as the warrior's morning song, and it begins with a praise, in which he adored God and asks God to gird up his strength for the conflicts he faces, and ends with a call summoning him to the battle.

Psalm 109 is a psalm that is difficult to read, let alone imagine being sung in the temple. Though David often cried out for rescue, he would only want the conversion of his worst enemies so they would not invoke curses such as we read here. However, there are evildoers in the world who are hardened and irredeemable adversaries of all that is good and of the Lord Himself. We cannot find it in ourselves to wish them well, but only that they will be overthrown and destroyed. We who have been saved by grace and taught to love and pray for our enemies may have a hard time uttering such words. It helps to realize this song has a spirit of prophecy of the enemies of Jesus rather than David, with the foresight of the certain destruction of all the unapologetic, unashamed, and habitual doers of evil.

Even the most loving and forgiving of people burn with indignation when they see or hear of the monstrous and unspeakable evil perpetrated upon women, children, and all innocent victims. Anger is stirred in our hearts when the good, harmless, and most gentle in this world suffer cruel oppression and wickedness. It is because of our Christian spirit and because we would wish only good upon all people that we cry out in righteous indignation for justice to fall against these hostile and malevolent humans. In reading this soul-shuddering psalm, we can take comfort in the foresight of the certain scorn and destruction of all those unyielding enemies of God and humankind.

Have you witnessed such evil in this world that it stirs up a revengeful spirit within you? Has this same wickedness touched you or your loved ones personally? Be careful, but let your righteous indignation take you to the court of heaven to lodge your complaints. Take your appeals to the Supreme Judge, asking Him to help you. Place your trust in Him, for He says those who have committed unimaginable harm to you or your precious loved ones are already set aside for His judgment. They will not escape His justice.

Lord, I praise You for Your sovereign promises of the deliverance of Your children and the sure destruction of those who torment the innocent people of this world. You gather the scattered, free the captive, heal the tormented, and rescue those in danger and distress. I praise and thank You that not only will the wicked be judged, but the righteous will be saved.

Be a morning warrior. Praise God for His works and His ways. Ask for strength for the battles of life as you join the fellow soldiers in the fray, anticipating victory and the trampling down of enemies.

Persevere in Praise

Praise the LORD.

Praise the LORD, you his servants,
   praise the name of the LORD.
Let the name of the LORD be praised,
   both now and forevermore.
From the rising of the sun to the place where it sets,
   the name of the LORD is to be praised.
—*Psalm 113:1–3*

M ost of the time David, whether in a cave or on the throne, began his prayerful songs with praise. If not at the beginning, his believing praise is found somewhere in the psalm, even if he seemed to be choking it out through tears. Psalm 110 urges the praise of Jesus as our Redeemer, Prophet, Priest, and King. Psalm 111 urges the praise for the great works of God and His glory in them. Psalm 112 urges the praise of God and His commands and the great bounty of privileges available to those who seek obedience. Psalm 114 is a song sung at the end of the Passover supper, praising and acknowledging God's power and goodness in what He did for Israel, and further, the greater work of the cross, our salvation and redemption by Christ.

Above all, the invitation to praise is greatest in Psalm 113. We get the idea that praising God is a very pressing and necessary duty. This is a calling of God's people, His servants, to praise Him. It is their duty and work, though it be joyful work, for they know Him and receive so much of His favor and blessings. It is a calling from generation to generation and from all places, now and always, from the rising of the sun to its setting. The invitation urges looking up with faith and awe at all His heavenly glory, and looking down at all the abundance He extends to His creation. He stoops down and humbles Himself to visit and order the affairs of humankind. God chooses to employ the least likely people to do His great work, lifting the low to high places. Sometimes He settles the barren woman in her home as a happy mother of children.

If there are countless reasons for praising God, why does it seem so hard to do sometimes, and why do we forget? It's easier when things are going well, when the sun is rising and life is round, full, and fruitful, for praising God magnifies those blessings. However, it is more difficult, even when you love and trust the Lord, to find words of praise when the sun is setting and life remains hollow and barren. We must persevere in praise even when it's the most difficult. It is through counting our blessings we begin to see that God has not abandoned us, but is still present and working in the middle of our difficult seasons. Maybe you have been waiting for the happiness of parenthood in the most literal sense, or maybe your life has simply been empty and fruitless. These are the suffering seasons, when praise can only be choked through hot tears. Take comfort in knowing there is a particularly sweet joy when His blessings come, in His perfect way, to those who have long been barren and waiting.

Lord, as Your humble servant I praise Your holy name. I will praise You now and forevermore. I will praise You when the light of the sun touches my face and shines brightest on me, and I will praise You when the sun sets into dusk. I will praise You when life is full and fruitful, and I will praise You when life is lean and barren. For You are a sovereign God, high and lifted up, but You graciously stooped down to save me. You will surely stoop down again to order the affairs of my life.

When it feels as if God isn't hearing you or coming to your rescue, count your blessings. Soon your mouth will be full of humble praise and your heart with tender hope.

Better Than Lemonade

Blessed is he who comes in the name of the Lord.
    From the house of the Lord we bless you.
The Lord is God,
    and he has made his light shine on us.
With boughs in hand, join in the festal procession
    up to the horns of the altar.

You are my God, and I will praise you;
    you are my God, and I will exalt you.

Give thanks to the Lord, for he is good;
    his love endures forever.
—*Psalm 118:26–29*

Read Psalms 115–118

When *life gives you lemons, make lemonade.* This is a popular phrase encouraging a person to make the best out of the difficult situations we experience in life. The encouragement is to look for the life lesson to help a person cope and give a person strength and knowledge to better face future challenges. However, when God gave David lemons, he didn't stop at optimistically searching for the good in the struggles he encountered. His end goal and focus was to seek and find God amid these sour seasons. Our Lord is the One who brings us through these experiences, drawing us closer to Himself and His plan for us. We must be careful not to make the focus of the Christian life about having the best life experiences. Our focus instead should be the life of Christ and our best life in Him.

Psalm 118 is another psalm most likely written by David after facing many trials but now taking his place on his anointed, kingly throne. He gave thanks to the Redeemer for his rescue from oppression and for his advancement as king of Israel. He invited everyone to praise God for His goodness and to trust God, making note of his own experiences of receiving God's tender mercy and mighty power. Even when things were going well, David was sensible of his obligations. He knew he was not his own self-made man and king, but bought with a price and appointed with a purpose. Therefore, he was more driven than ever to praise God, for he knew his whole success depended upon Him. Psalm 115 reveals the heart of a psalmist when the church was faced with persecution by its enemies with insolent mocking and the dismissing of the former miracles of God. Though it surely grieved God's people that God would be so dishonored, they did not worry themselves over their own persecution as children of God, but rather they called on God to vindicate His own name. The psalmist exhorted the people to trust God and bless His name and to make sure He was not robbed of His rightful praise. Psalm 116 is another thanksgiving psalm where we find the psalmist grateful for experiencing the goodness of God in and through the great distresses that nearly drove him to utter despair. Psalm 117 is short and sweet, but full to the brim with the encouragement of all mankind to praise the name of the Lord.

David and all the psalmists surely desired their lemons to be turned to lemonade, but after searching themselves through and through, they realized there wasn't anything in and of themselves that merited the comfort, support, and benefits of God. Instead they asked God to deliver them and grant their requests for His name's sake, that the glory and praise due Him might be maintained. When all other hopes fail, when life is one big sour season, God is our only hope to bring us through while revealing more of Himself, His love, and His faithfulness, in the process.

Lord, please help me to keep my eyes fixed on You and Your purposes for me rather than simply trying to find something good in my situations. If lemonade is my only goal, I might miss Your presence, teaching, and the ministry obligations You have appointed for me. Lord, I praise You, for great is Your love and faithfulness even when I am without merit to receive it. You have delivered my soul from death, my eyes from tears, and my feet from stumbling. Your love endures forever.

Let us not be satisfied with only finding the good in the difficult and messy work of life, but with finding the goodness of God in it as well.

Hide His Word in Your Heart

I have hidden your word in my heart
    that I might not sin against you.
Praise be to you, Lord;
    teach me your decrees.
With my lips I recount
    all the laws that come from your mouth.
I rejoice in following your statutes
    as one rejoices in great riches.
I meditate on your precepts
    and consider your ways.
I delight in your decrees;
    I will not neglect your word.
—*Psalm 119:11–16*

Read Psalm 119

P salm 119 is the longest psalm and the longest chapter in the Bible. Within the psalm there are eight couplets, each beginning with one of the twenty-two letters of the Hebrew alphabet in order. One could easily spend a lifetime digging and sifting through the treasures of Psalm 119, but its overarching theme is the Word of God and that the Word of God is a priority to God. Some of the main themes concerning the Bible speak of God's authority. The justice of His commands, ordinances, precepts, statutes, and judgment is rooted in His own character. God's meticulous laws reveal how He cares about every detail concerning His will for how His people should live in obedience. The Bible bears witness and gives testimony to what God has done and is doing, and His divine ways are contrasted with humankind's ways. God's Word declares the infallible permanence of Scripture and is not filled with optional suggestions for the believer. Some have questioned the inerrancy of Scripture, but even some of those who believe it is the authoritative Word of God doubt that it is fully relevant or sufficient to apply and minister to these sophisticated modern times. People, even many Christians, turn to other resources lacking in biblical truth to help meet their mental, emotional, practical, and spiritual needs.

In verses 9–16, as well as other verses, we find David declaring he will seek God with all his heart and asking God to not let him stray from His Word and His commands. He hid the Word in his heart that he might always have close access to it when he needed it for wisdom and direction, that he might not sin against God. Just as Jesus used the Scripture against the Enemy in the desert, David gave praise and glory to God, asking God to teach him His precepts that he would know how to follow and serve God faithfully, pleasing God and being blessed by Him. David recounted all the laws of God and had the testimony of referring to them when he was king, but also when he was in regular conversation with people. He used his biblical knowledge for good, and he was a fountain always sharing his knowledge with others. He rejoiced in God's statutes as one who rejoices in accumulating wealth. He took constant pleasure in communion with God, meditating on His precepts and delighting in His decrees.

If you know God and love God, but are going through a difficult season where you cannot see Him clearly, hear Him clearly, or feel His active presence, take your search to His Word. His voice will give you hope and stability. It will guide you and help you walk uprightly down a righteous path. God will use His living water to revive you, saturating your dry bones. Meditate on God's Word, delight in it, and hide it in your heart. God will use it to speak truth and comfort to you and keep you safe and secure.

Lord, I will open my Bible more diligently and put my hope in Your rich and unfailing Word. I will seek Your precepts, decrees, and statutes, that I may be refreshed and gain understanding, but also that I may walk in a way that honors and pleases You. I will join the psalmist in saying, "how sweet are Your words to my taste, sweeter than honey to my mouth" (v. 103). Your Word is a lamp unto my feet and a light unto my path.

Have you neglected God's Word? Has it been your delight and passion? Since the Word of God is a top priority to God, endeavor to make it a top priority to you.

Where Your Help Comes From

I lift up my eyes to the mountains—
    where does my help come from?
My help comes from the LORD,
    the Maker of heaven and earth.
—*Psalm 121:1-2*

Read Psalms 120-124

P salms 120–124 are the first five of a special grouping of psalms called the Songs of Ascent. Four psalms are attributed to David, one to Solomon, and ten are anonymous. While these songs might not have been originally written for these purposes, over time they have been grouped together. Many scholars believe these "songs of going up" were adopted as songs of pilgrimage and would be sung by the Jewish people who were making their way to Jerusalem, the city on the hill, for the three main Jewish festivals. Some traditions suggest the Levite priests also sang these fifteen songs as they ascended each of the fifteen steps of the temple. Some also make a spiritual connection suggesting these songs are ascents of the soul, rising from lowest sorrow to the highest joy and going up from the valley of weeping unto the presence of God.[7]

In Psalm 120, the author bemoaned the dishonest, violent, peace-hating culture he felt doomed to live in. Though he had tried living in peace with these lying, false brethren, they constantly tormented him. He called out in distress, longing to be rescued and to leave this place far behind. In Psalm 121 he lifted His eyes up to the hills, asking where his help came from, then acknowledged his help came from the Lord, the Maker of heaven and earth. The journey away from weeping had begun, and he comforted himself knowing the God who never sleeps was watching over him. God would protect him, not let him slip into sin, and keep him safe as he traveled forward. Psalm 122 finds the pilgrim arriving at the gates of Jerusalem, marveling at its beauty and majesty, excited to go further up and further in to praise the name of the Lord. Like someone arriving home again, for the sake of his family and friends, he prayed for the peace and safety of Jerusalem, seeking forever the city's prosperity. In Psalm 123, he lifted his eyes to see God and His throne. He acknowledged his full dependence on God; as a slave looks to the hand of his master or a maid looks to the hand of her mistress, so too did he look to the hand of God for refuge and mercy. In Psalm 124 he recounted how God had rescued Israel, giving God all the credit and glory. If not for His mercy and deliverance, they would have been swallowed alive, completely engulfed, and torn by the teeth of their enemies.

Are you weary of dwelling in Meshek? Tired of the lies and violence you see in the world? Maybe the dishonesty and cruelty are even closer to home. Maybe the deceit and destruction are in your own life and heart. Let the utter dissatisfaction of the brokenness in which you are living send you on a pilgrimage from the valley of weeping to the presence of God. Know where your help comes from, the Maker of heaven and earth. The God who never sleeps will watch over you, protect you, and keep your foot from slipping as you journey further up and further in to the presence of God.

Lord, I am so tired of living like this, but I don't know where to go. I am standing at Your gates. Can I come to You? Will You please guide me and protect me? Will You please lead me to a better place, a beautiful place high on a hill where I can finally find peace within my walls?

Do you need to leave? Is it time to go? Lift your eyes to the hills; your help comes from the Lord, the Maker of heaven and earth.

The Only Firm Foundation

Restore our fortunes, LORD,
   like streams in the Negev.
Those who sow with tears
   will reap with songs of joy.
Those who go out weeping,
   carrying seed to sow,
will return with songs of joy,
   carrying sheaves with them.
—*Psalm 126:4-6*

Read Psalms 125–129

T he journey upward continues in Psalms 125–129. Psalm 125 is a song of divine confidence. Those who trust in the Lord will forever be secure, and the end result of faith is always a blessing. Though it may seem as if darkness rules the day, God surrounds His people like an immovable mountain range. Our hope can be sure, not because we are strong, but because our God is. In fact, if the scepter of power passed from the wicked to the good, it wouldn't take long for them to become wicked too. We all need the King of kings to intervene in our lives and govern us that we might not give in to crooked ways.

In Psalm 126 we encounter great rejoicing in the recounting and remembering of those once in captivity being delivered. It was a dream come true! They were filled with joy; laughter had returned. All the people in the surrounding nations couldn't help but notice and proclaim that the Lord had done great things for them. The tears they had sown reaped for them songs of joy. Psalm 127 is the Builder's Psalm, written by Solomon. It's quite fitting and appropriate that the builder of the holy house of God would be remembered by the people making their pilgrimage to the temple. Solomon reminds us that builders of houses and cities build in vain without the Lord. He is the only firm foundation. Solomon declares that everything, from our families to our work, is all in vain unless the Lord builds it and protects it. Psalm 128 is an obvious step up from the last, which declared how a house should be built and revealed what it should then become. The wisdom of God brings joy, peace, and prosperity. The blessing of the Lord now goes beyond the children to the children's children, beginning as arrows and now as olive shoots. Psalm 129 is a lament of someone looking back over a long season of affliction. Though he had been greatly oppressed, his resolve remained strong, and his faith remained steadfast in the Lord.

What do think about when you hear Solomon say that you get up early and stay up late, toiling in vain? Are you looking back over a long period of misfortune? Are you tired of trying to build up your life only to watch it crumble, realizing you can't keep it from collapsing? Do you desire a peaceful, happy home and important, fruitful work? These psalms encourage us to work diligently, love sacrificially, and train our children to walk with God, but God wants to keep us from fretful living, excessive labor, and stressful anxiety. We cannot obtain and secure sustaining contentment, joy, and prosperity on our own steam, because these are the blessings of God.

Lord, there is certainly something inside me that feels I need to take control of everything, but Lord, I am tired and at my wits' end. I don't know what to do to get back on track, and that scares me. This dark cloud has settled in for so long. I miss the bright, warm sunshine. I miss being happy. Please intervene, show me Your will, and give me strength to change what I need to change and trust You with all the rest.

Has a dark cloud settled over you? Remember God surrounds you as your Protector. Let Him intervene and govern your life; then you can count on Him to turn your weeping into songs of joy.

Songs of Ascent

Praise the L<small>ORD</small>, all you servants of the L<small>ORD</small>
   who minister by night in the house of the L<small>ORD</small>.
Lift up your hands in the sanctuary
   and praise the L<small>ORD</small>.

May the L<small>ORD</small> bless you from Zion,
   he who is the Maker of heaven and earth.
—*Psalm 134*

Read Psalms 130–134

The fifteen Songs of Ascent are sometimes divided into three groups of five and are compared to three ascents of the soul and spiritual life. Regular and steady references to souls in trouble and spiritual lives in danger can be found in Psalms 120–124. Psalms 125–129 begin to reveal and solidify a soulful trust and a spiritual confidence in God, and Psalms 130–134 lead the soul and spirit into direct communion with the Lord. The writer of Psalm 130 began in the depths of repentance, but soon climbed to the highest level of confidence in God's mercy. If God were to keep a record of our sins, no one would be able to enter, let alone stand in His presence. This psalmist knew he needed God's mercy and then trusted God to give it to him.

Psalm 131 is short in words and yet it soars. This is the heart of David, who, through his sifting and sanctifying journey upward, was weaned from his idols and insecurities. His will was whatever God willed, and his hope was in God alone. David's spirit was humble, submissive, and finally quieted, but still wholly confident. Psalm 132 begins lowly with affliction but ascends all the way to the throne. The Lord remembered David and his hardships. The Lord remembered His oaths and vows to David and His people, sympathized with them, accepted them, and helped them. Psalm 133 is a far cry from the start of the pilgrimage, which was full of loneliness, war, and lamentations, arriving now at peace and pleasantness. David, knowing well the bitterness of broken relationships, reveled in how good it felt when his brothers and sisters came together in unity, and now in the presence and the blessing of the Lord. The last step was an invitation to bless the Lord. All the servants of the Lord who have ascended the holy hill from all different paths and experiences praised the Lord. In the sanctuary, they lifted high their hands and worshipped God with one elevated voice.

The Christian life is a challenging climb, further up and further in, and the Songs of Ascent are a precious treasure. Depth, prayer, conviction, weeping, sowing, trusting, seeking, expecting, hoping, waiting, watching, longing, assurance, presence, worshiping; are you climbing these steps? Are you hearing God's instruction and encouragement in these songs and wondering if this is just what you need? Are you looking back and holding on to better days, painting those memories in favorable shades of flattering colors? Rather than asking God to take you back there, look to an ongoing relationship with God moving you forward to a new and better life and future glory.

Lord, this is the first step, where the healing begins. Where does my help come from? My help comes from You, the Maker of heaven and earth. My heart and my soul, I give You control. Remember me and all the hardships I've endured. Dwell with me forever, sit enthroned over my life, and bless me with Your abundant provisions. Lead me from the depths of distress to Your city on the hill, that I might lift my hands high and worship You until that day when I take that last step and You lead this pilgrim home.

These psalms rise out of the depths of anguish to the heights of confident assurance and rejoicing. Treasures are often buried in deep places. They might not have ever been found had God not ever cast us down.

Enduring Love

Give thanks to the God of heaven.
His love endures forever.
—*Psalm 136:26*

Read Psalms 135–137

Have you ever noticed praying and worship are much easier to do when you are living in peace and security, but much more difficult when that peace and security has been breached and violated by opposition and conflict? Psalm 135 is a mosaic song of selections from other psalms carefully arranged, producing a new work of art—a song one might easily sing in times of peace. God is praised for His goodness, love, greatness, righteous judgments, unchanging character, and love for His people. Nothing can be more worth repeating than God's enduring, merciful love, and in times of security, Psalm 136 would be a pleasant and agreeable melody. The author of Psalm 136 is unknown, but this praise and worship song was sung in Solomon's temple and by the armies of Jehoshaphat as they marched into victory in the Desert of Tekoa, but then we come upon weeping and lamenting songs, such as Psalm 137.

Are the last two verses of Psalm 137 difficult for you to read? Do you bristle when you come across these prayers for violence? The words are undeniably harsh, but the burning indignation might be better understood within context. The composer of this song had watched Israel's foremost archenemies burn down his temple and tear down his city all the way to its foundation. He had witnessed all the women in his city being ravished and all the children being slain in front of their parents. Both the words and the picture are uncomfortable to take in, but the sentiment pouring through the psalmist's fiery anger and sadness can be better comprehended. This is a song written by a grieving patriot with an unfading love of his country and an undying contempt for its levelers and his captors. They cruelly mocked him and his fellow musicians, demanding them now, after the horror they had inflicted upon these innocent people, to pick up their instruments and sing songs of joy to them. How could they sing as they were being carried off to Babylon, traveling farther and farther away from their beloved home? The only sound they could utter was the moaning and wailing song of captivity and exile.

If you are living in peace, give thanks to the Lord, for He is good. His love endures forever. Has your peace been violated? Give thanks to God. His love endures forever. If your security has been breached, give thanks to the Lord, who led His people through the desert, struck down mighty kings, and gave their land as an inheritance. His love endures forever. If you are so sad and angry you can hardly see straight, let alone pray and sing, start by giving thanks to the Lord, who remembers us in our low estate and frees us from our captors and exile. His love endures forever.

Lord, sometimes it's so easy for me to come to You and pray and go to church and raise my hands high before You. But other times, when the Enemy has destroyed everything and he's holding me captive, my voice trembles and I can't get the words out. Only sad, hot tears surface. I can't lift my arms or open my hands because they are curled into tight, angry fists. In those times please listen to the moaning hymn in my broken heart. It's quiet, but it still acknowledges and praises You.

Whether in peace or captivity, whether out loud or from the moan of your heart, acknowledge God and give thanks. His love endures forever.

Perfect Justice

May slanderers not be established in the land;
　　may disaster hunt down the violent.

I know that the LORD secures justice for the poor
　　and upholds the cause of the needy.
Surely the righteous will praise your name,
　　and the upright will live in your presence.
—*Psalm 140:11-13*

When you witness abhorrent and reprehensible acts committed, one upon another, are you tempted to think God must not be watching? The times we are living in are replete with backbiting and infighting, very similar to David's descriptions of his time. Psalm 139 is a psalm of David, speaking once again of the omniscient nature of God. If God is everywhere, then He knows everything. If God is the Creator, then He knows everyone. There is no escape from God. Not only is He watching and listening, He's paying attention. Nothing gets by Him. David was a man of war and a man who experienced numerous afflictions at the hands of his enemies, but he always took his complaints and cries of injustice straight to the Lord. David remembered that the battle against all the chaos, vile mocking, and the reprehensible assaults of this world belonged to the Lord. He knew it was God who secured justice for the poor and upheld the cause of the needy. The Lord maintains His just cause, and in a day when real and true justice is ill-defined, murky, and hard to find, there is great assurance and peace for those who acknowledge the omniscience of God, knowing He will execute His perfect justice upon those who need it.

What about you? Are you speaking up in these times of injustice? Though there is a time to be silent, we see in Psalm 138 there is also a time to speak up. David was resolved and confident, always prepared to own and confess his God. He was never ashamed to be affiliated with God or God's edicts, decrees, and commands. He was always at the ready to proselytize, whether it be to kings or nations, until every man, woman, and child sang praises of allegiance to God and lived in the peace, freedom, and salvation He offers. There is a time to keep silent, when the treasures of God will fall upon deaf ears, but there is also a time to speak up—a time to bear witness and give testimony and share the rich and healing message of Christ with those who are poor in spirit and hurting.

Are you ever tempted to believe God isn't paying attention to what you're doing, that He's not listening to what you're saying, and that He hasn't seen what you've been up to? If He made you and already knows all your days, then trying to hide from Him is futile. Better yet, let the beauty of this truth sink in: God knows everything about you, even more than you know and understand about yourself. He knows your innermost self, even the darkest areas of your heart, and He still pursues you and wants to have a relationship with you. You might as well submit yourself to Him, let Him search and clean up your heart, and then follow Him down a righteous path to everlasting holiness.

Lord, I praise You and I thank You. You created my inmost being and knit me together in my mother's womb. Your eyes saw my unformed body, and all the days of my life were already ordained for me and written in Your book. Lord, fulfill Your purpose for me, teaching me to speak when I need to speak and to be silent when I need to be silent. Search me and know my heart and lead me to walk in righteousness.

If you can really start to wrap your mind around the truth that nothing about you or this world escapes the knowledge and attention of God, it will become a humbling influence to seek better His holiness, but it will also become a great comfort.

A Sovereign God

Answer me quickly, LORD;
    my spirit fails.
Do not hide your face from me
    or I will be like those who go down to the pit.
Let the morning bring me word of your unfailing love,
    for I have put my trust in you.
Show me the way I should go,
    for to you I entrust my life.
—*Psalm 143:7-8*

Have you ever been in a season where you have had to make some difficult choices? Are you in one now? No matter what you decide, it's going to pinch and hurt either way? All three psalms here are written by David. Again, we encounter a burdened man with an utterly overwhelmed spirit. Most all of his compositions sprang out of the fountains of the hard stuff of life. David cried to God. He wanted God to hear him and come to him right away. His petitions were lit on fire by his sincerity, rising to God like burning incense. He raised his hands, heaved, and waved his pleas and appeals like an evening sacrifice, his faith reaching God as a sweet-smelling aroma. No matter how desperate and complicated life became, he kept his eyes fixed on the sovereign Lord, taking refuge in God's unlimited and ultimate power.

When David was pushed back into a confined and restricted cave, tears and prayers were his only tools and weapons. He survived, not by keeping all his troubles there with him and stewing over them, but by crying them out and lifting them up. David took comfort in knowing the sovereign God knew exactly where he was, who he was, and what he was going through. David knew a dark and confined cave dwelling couldn't possibly be what God had for him. God made promises to him and appointed David to a life of godly purpose. He pleaded with God to give him a quick answer because he wasn't sure about what to do and he didn't know where to go from here. He hoped to wake up in the morning to God's lovingkindness and clear guidance. David lifted his whole soul, that God might take it in His hands and form it Himself into His perfect will for David's life. Not only did David need God to show him His will, he needed power to walk in it. He prayed that God would enliven him in his devotion. He needed God to change his mind and his heart. Finally, he prayed that God would, in His own way and His own timing, clear out a path to his anointed life.

Have you been living in tight quarters? Do you hear God calling you to step out of that close-packed, dense, and overgrown life, but you are hesitant because you know you can't take everything with you if you do? Is the one thing God is asking you to leave behind your dream? Is He asking you to step out in faith and trust Him? Can you find faith enough to let go and walk away?

Lord, I call to You; hear me and answer me quickly. I think I already know what You want me to do, but it's hard to let go. I lift my whole soul to You; please conform it to Your will, but please be gentle. I will fix my eyes upon You, for You are my sovereign Lord. Let the morning bring me word of your unfailing love, for I have put my trust in You.

Can you hear God asking you to walk away? Will you lay your dream down on the altar as a sacrifice of trust to a sovereign God with limitless power? Do you believe He will, in His own way and His own timing, clear a path to your anointed life?

Victory Is Coming

The LORD is trustworthy in all he promises
    and faithful in all he does.
The LORD upholds all who fall
    and lifts up all who are bowed down.
The eyes of all look to you,
    and you give them their food at the proper time.
You open your hand
    and satisfy the desires of every living thing.

The LORD is righteous in all his ways
    and faithful in all he does.
—*Psalm 145:13–17*

Read Psalms 144–146

The book of Psalms winds down with songs of praise. At the end of the day, praise is the culmination. David decided no matter what happened, he was going to praise the Lord. He would make it his work and his delight to exalt our God the King, forever and ever. Every day He would esteem and elevate His name, for He is most worthy of praise, and his greatness cannot be fathomed. The Lord is gracious and compassionate, slow to anger and rich in love (145:8). He is ready and eager to pour out His blessings more than we are ready to ask for and enjoy them. He is ready and eager to pour out His compassion and forgiveness more than we are ready to repent and receive it and live in freedom. The Lord is good to all and has compassion on all He has made. The stubborn and unyielding exclude themselves from His abundant riches. Sometimes we are afflicted with sickness or hardships that seem to be dragging us to the grave, but then His right hand upholds us and we are miraculously saved. Even when we fall, He quickly picks us back up again. Those who are bowed down by oppression, only God can raise up. Though we may fall, we are never utterly cast down or forsaken. Those who put their trust in men and women will surely be disappointed, but those whose hope is in the Lord will be blessed and happy. Do you sense the goodness of God marching and advancing you to triumph? Can you sense the quiet calm that comes with victory? Are you beginning to see with better clarity? Is the scene coming into focus? Can you see the prosperity coming? Can you picture your sons growing wiser and better, your daughters firmly established? Can you picture your barns overflowing and your flocks greatly increasing? Can you imagine yourself living in plenty, happy and useful, able to be charitable and generous with your family, friends, and neighbors? Can you imagine uninterrupted peace, no more hiding in caves, no more moaning songs from captive lands, and no more cries of distress? Blessed are the people of whom this is true; blessed are the people whose God is the Lord.

Lord, praise be to You who are my Rock, my Fortress, my Stronghold, my Shield, and my Refuge. You are faithful to all Your promises. Uphold me; don't let me fall. You are loving to all You have made; I lift my eyes to see Your goodness. I will not put my trust in princes or mortal men who cannot save. My hope is in You, the Maker of heaven and earth. I can sense my victory coming. Thank You for Your boundless grace and mercy. Great are You and worthy of praise.

All the riches of the world cannot make us happy unless the Creator of the world is our God.

Raised from Ruin

Praise the Lord.

How good it is to sing praises to our God,
　　how pleasant and fitting to praise Him!

The Lord builds up Jerusalem;
　　he gathers the exiles of Israel.
He heals the brokenhearted
　　and binds up their wounds.
He determines the number of stars
　　and calls them each by name.
Great is our Lord and mighty in power;
　　his understanding has no limit.
The Lord sustains the humble
　　but casts the wicked to the ground.
—*Psalm 147:1–6*

Read Psalms 147–150

T he book of Psalms begins by revealing two ways to approach life and live in it, describing the difference between those who have reverence for the Lord and His Word and those who do not. The book of Psalms ends with the joy, elation, and delight of those who have devoted their lives to God and the exaltation of Him. We have been called over and over to praise the Lord as the God of creation, for He is very great and the God of grace and mercy, for He rescues and comforts His people. All the creatures of the earth are called to praise God to the depths of their capacity, to the maximum amount they can contain. It is by divine design, not only to bring God what is due Him, but it is for our pleasure and health as well. Our happy duty becomes its own reward.

God is the object of our praise because He takes care of His own people. He builds up Jerusalem and gathers the exiles of Israel. He raises the city back up from its ruins. He builds up the church, being its foundation and cornerstone. He builds up His children, growing them from their small beginnings. He heals the brokenhearted, those who are crushed by life's circumstances and those who have thrown themselves into a life of sin, destruction, and despair. He is a gentle Healer, who whispers peace to them as He applies soothing balm to their open and throbbing wounds. He speaks the comfort of reconciliation and assurance of clemency as he binds and stitches their life back together.

Are you starting over again? Are you starting small? Zechariah 4:10 exhorts us not to despise small beginnings, for the Lord rejoices just to see the work begin. Don't be tempted to think this little start won't produce great increase. You will not labor in vain if the Lord builds you up. If you plant your tiny seed of faith in Jesus alone and water it with earnest prayer, nothing will be impossible for you. His gracious and powerful providence will go before you. Just as David danced before God with all his might, make it your duty and reward to praise your Redeemer. Own God's name and sing aloud; sing with all your heart and without shame. Sing new songs, one written for every occasion. Praise God in private, in public, and in joyful chorus within the body of Christ.

Lord, the work is just beginning. Raise me from my ruins; become my foundation and my cornerstone. Grow me from these small beginnings. Whisper peace, comfort, and reconciliation as You gently apply Your soothing balm to my heart. Stitch my life back together again using Your pattern. I praise You to the depths of my capacity. Thank You for Your relentless pursuit of me and for Your never-ending presence and purpose. Take me and build me up into holy perfection. Let the heavens praise You! Let the earth praise You! Let everything that has breath praise the Lord!

> **Let praising become the air you breathe, the air you can't live without, and the breathing of your innermost soul. While you have breath, praise the Lord, and then praise the Lord with your last breath.**

Notes

1. Steve Farrar, *Gettin' There: A Passage Through the Psalms* (Colorado Springs, CO: Multnomah, 2007), 201.

2. C. Hassell Bullock, *Encountering the Book of Psalms: A Literary and Theological Introduction* (Grand Rapids, MI: Baker, 2001), 23.

3. Matthew Henry, *Zondervan NIV Matthew Henry Commentary* (Grand Rapids, MI: Zondervan, 1999); Charles J. Ellicott, *Ellicott's Bible Commentary for English Readers Volume 3* (Harrington, DE: Delmarva Publications, 2015).

4. Charles H. Spurgeon, *The Treasury of David: Spurgeon's Classic Work on the Psalms* (Grand Rapids, MI: Kregel Publications, 1976), 78.

5. Ibid., 213.

6. Christopher Klein, "9 Things You May Not Know About 'The Star-Spangled Banner,'" History.com, September 12, 2014, http://www.history.com/news/9-things-you-may-not-know-about-the-star-spangled-banner.

7. Eugene H. Peterson, *A Long Obedience in the Same Direction: Discipleship in an Instant Society* (Downers Grove, IL: InterVarsity Press, 2000).